D1180470

28. FEB. 1973
22. AUG. 1975

-3 MAR. 1975

23. JUN. 1975

14 JUL 1975

-4. DEC. 1976

14. I. 77

MONTHLY LOAN

-4. NOV. 1977

28. NOV. 1977

28. FEB. 1978

22 March

-1. APR. 1978

18 May.

10. MAR. 1978

MONTHLY LOAN

-8. JUN. 1978

20. OCT. 1978

MONTHLY LOAN

17. OCT. 1978

21. SEP. 1979

MONTHLY LOAN

22. SEP. 1975

22. DEC. 1975

6. MAR. 1976

11. JUL. 1976

AUTHOR BLAKEMORE, K.

TITLE Book of Gold

CLASS No. 739.22

BOOK No. 97203415

This book must be returned on or before the date shown above
to the Library from which it was borrowed
LANCASHIRE COUNTY LIBRARY
143 CORPORATION STREET, PRESTON, PR1 8RH

LANCASHIRE LIBRARIES
3 0118 06341827 5

THE BOOK OF GOLD

The story of man's obsession with gold, and the
artefacts which his craftsmen – the goldsmiths –
have created in the 'noble' metal from the dawn
of civilisation onwards.

The Book of
GOLD

Kenneth Blakemore

This book has been made possible through the
co-operation of Benson & Hedges Ltd.

n
November Books
London

Published by November Books Limited, 23–9 Emerald Street, London WC1N 3QL.

Text filmset by Yendall & Company Limited, Riscatype House, 22–5 Red Lion Court, Fleet Street, London EC4.

Printed by Drukkerij de Lange/Van Leer NV, Deventer, Netherlands.

Colour printed by Jay Print (Leicester) Limited, Ireton Avenue, Leicester LE4 7EY.

Bound by Webb, Son & Company Limited, 303 Chase Road, Southgate, London N14 6JB.

Copyright © November Books Limited 1971.   ISBN 0233 96223 9
This edition is not for sale in the USA or Canada.

Picture Credits

Colour: Trustees of the British Museum 19, 20 (bottom), 54, 71 (top), 72, 90, 181; Bernard Cox 3, 53; Christies frontispiece, 89, 120, 139, 140-1, 152, 182-3; Michael Holford 130; Omega Collection 165; Sotheby and Co. 117, 118-9, 143; Spectrum/Tomsich 129; Government of United Arab Republic 20 (top); Victoria and Albert Museum 71 (bottom), 107, 108, 151, 161, 163. Black and white: Aachen Treasury, photographer Ann Münchow-Lepper 99, 100; Ashmolean Museum, Oxford 109, 220; Griffith Institute 27, 57; Controller of Her Brittanic Majesty's Stationery Office 176, 185; N. Bloom and Son 44 (right), 153 (top); Trustees of the British Museum 60, 61, 73, 77 (bottom), 90, 95 (right), 101, 104, 112, photographer Angelo Hornak 68, 74, 75, 79, 82 (bottom), 91, Treasures of Romania Exhibition 48, 49, 65 (right), 81 (top), 94 (top right and below), 95 (left); Cameo Corner 155, 156; Bernard Cox 66, 86; Christies 77 (top), 78, 88 (bottom), 92, 98, 158; Michael Holford 35, 128; Angelo Hornak 81 (bottom), 82 (top), 83; National Museum, Dublin 103, 105, 106; Public Archives of Canada 43, 44; Schmuckmuseum, Pforzheim, photographer G. Meyer 70, 85, 88, 121 (top left), photographer G. Wipfler 29, 84, 94, 96; Sotheby and Co. 121 (lower left and above right), 123, 166 (right); Twining Collection, Goldsmith's Hall 111, 187, Stencuy Graficky Zavod 189, Kunstverlag Anton Schroll 191, Edizione Muzie 194, Marburg 196; Government of United Arab Republic 56; Victoria and Albert Museum 96 (bottom), 97, 111 (right), 122, 131, 132, 133, 134, 135, 136, 150, 153, 154, 160, 166 (left); Messrs Wartski 147, 148, 165, 167, 168, 169; Worshipful Company of Goldsmiths 22, 23, 24, 114.

Colour illustration on page 1: *the mask found at Mycenae by Schliemann, who supposed it to be that of Agamemnon. National Museum, Athens.*
Frontispiece: *gold cup and cover of Charles II, made in 1671, with engraved coat of arms. This sold for £37,000 ($88,800) in London in 1969.*

Contents

To Norma and Sara Kate

A 16th-century goldsmith's workshop in Germany. Foreground, right: *a craftsman raises the body of a vessel over a rising stake;* foreground, left: *another hammers up repoussé decoration on a bowl.*

Introduction

Few of the earth's natural products have evoked so many different responses in man as gold. To the banker it represents the ultimate form of security. To the numismatist it is the metal from which the most beautiful coins have been struck. To the metallurgist it is an element with unique properties. To the craftsman it is the most rewarding of raw materials. To the economist it is still the final index of a nation's convertible wealth. And to most of mankind, it is the most potent and enduring symbol of private riches. Yet neither gold's economic importance, nor the metal's physical characteristics, fully explain the fascination it has always exerted over humanity – a fascination which remains as strong today as ever before.

Our own response to gold may stem in part from a lingering memory of its role in some of the earliest organised social groups. When these began to form – at least 10,000 years ago – gold was essentially mystical, associated with the sun, 'the giver of life'. The first rulers of those early societies used the metal, and its link with the life-giving source of all energy, to reinforce their claims to authority, giving it a central role in their coronation ceremonies to symbolise their divine right to power, a right they traced back to a common ancestry with the gods. To the Incas of Peru gold was nothing less than the 'sweat of the sun'. They believed their kings to be the direct descendants of the sun-god, honouring them in palaces which they sheathed with the precious metal that the god, in his generosity, had bestowed on the earth.

In ancient Egypt, too, a sun-god was the principal deity – Ra – whose progeny were the Egyptian kings and whose temples contained great golden discs, so that the Egyptians should never forget from where their rulers derived the authority to rule. (While none of these golden discs survive, symbolic suns appear on many of the jewels discovered by modern archaeologists in the tombs of such kings as Tutankhamun.) In fact, all of ancient Egypt's gold was royal property, and Ra's legacy was used not only in the temples, but for public display in the form of elaborate jewels – worn by the kings not for decoration but as formal badges of office. More important still, these jewels were talismans. On them were engraved the signs of Horus the Hawk, the vulture goddess Nekhbet, Uraeus, the serpent, and many more all placed there to protect the king from the inexplicable evils and dangers that threatened the life of even semi-divine beings.

Soon other kings in the ancient world were mirroring the splendour of Egypt's rulers. By 3000 B.C., in the valley of the Euphrates in Mesopotamia, the river's banks were clustered with city-states. Sir Leonard Woolley, carrying out a dig in 1927 on the site of one such city-state, discovered the famous death pits of the Sumerian kings and found them to be full of golden artefacts. His discovery at first shocked the sensibilities of his contemporaries because it also revealed the macabre funeral rites of the Sumerian peoples. When one of their kings died, his whole court — hand-maidens, soldiers, musicians and grooms — dressed as for a feast, formed a cortège and accompanied his corpse down into the grave. There, so that he could enjoy their company in the after-life, they were buried alive with him.

Yet when the initial repulsion felt by Woolley's colleagues towards these practices had passed, the golden objects in the graves began to be seen in a different light: superbly-wrought and remarkably sophisticated expressions of the goldsmith's art — their existence in such profusion all the more astonishing for the fact that the Sumerians had no gold within their own territories.

The adoption of gold as the symbol of state — and its use in the great royal households for every conceivable purpose from wall-coverings to drinking goblets — created a demand for the metal that increased with every decade. As each Egyptian king (like the Sumerian kings also) was buried with a large proportion of the golden treasures he had amassed during his lifetime, this demand was soon almost insatiable. Well before 5000 B.C. the alluvial deposits along the banks of the Nile were being systematically sifted for ore. But, rich as these deposits were, they still could not meet the needs of successive dynasties. And so, by the fourth millenium B.C., thousands of captive slaves were being sent to dig mines and extract reef gold from the hills along the Red Sea between Coptos and Berenice. Nubia, too, was raided for further supplies and soon Egyptian ships were scouring the entire known world for yet more.

Mysticism, authority, wealth — and scarcity. All have been constant characteristics of the precious metal from the beginnings of civilisation until today. Even gold's divine associations remained as the centuries passed. Golden statues of the gods stood in the shrines of ancient Greece. When the faithful entered the great Byzantine church of Hagia Sophia, they passed first through doors covered in thick gold sheathing; and then, inside, their eyes would be dazzled by the richness of the golden tapestries, the gift of emperor after emperor. And in the Christian church itself gold has been used—

in pure form or as plate – for sacred vessels, focussing the worshippers' attention on the symbolic 'supreme value' of the sacramental contents.

Accompanying the early demand for gold came an equally urgent need for craftsmen to work it. The result was the elevation of the goldsmith to an important, highly-prized and richly-rewarded position in the courts of the many kings who required not only vast supplies of the metal, but its fashioning into objects of increasing sophistication. As civilisation spread throughout the Middle East and along the shores of the Mediterranean, goldsmiths found more and more employment in fulfilling royal commissions. They flourished in Babylon, in Minoan Crete, in Troy, Mycenae, Persia and Etruria. By the first millenium B.C. they were practising their craft in civilisations thousands of miles across the ocean which separated Europe from the American land-mass. In Peru, Colombia, Yucatan, the obsession with gold – and the tangible gleaming magnificence it gave to the courts of kings – was as intense as it had ever been in Egypt. And, as always, the goldsmith was there to reflect, interpret and create in metal the royal wishes.

In about 560 B.C. yet another use was found for gold. For a long time before this, gold, because the supply was never equal to the demand, had been readily accepted in exchange for goods and service. Now King Croesus of Lydia was to formalise the role of gold as a medium of exchange. In the middle of the 6th century B.C. he ordered the first gold coins to be struck. These gold staters bore his heraldic device, the facing heads of a lion and a bull, which guaranteed their value. As a result gold gradually became the measure of individual and national wealth. A man who had gold in his coffer could purchase luxuries from the four corners of the earth. A nation with gold in its treasury was a power to be respected and feared. Henceforward gold, as the basis of economic life, was to have an immeasurable influence on the course of history.

It has decided the fate of nations. It has been the underlying reality behind the hypocritical excuses for conquest. Individual men in their tens of thousands have been exploited in the pursuit of gold. Men have died for it and men have been murdered for it. In the 16th century, Spain destroyed the Inca civilisation of Peru to gain gold. 'Get gold – humanely if you can', the Spanish king had instructed his *conquistadores*. But the men who followed Pizarro and Cortés were 'irresponsible individuals, soldiers of fortune, desperate adventurers, who entered on conquest as a game, which they were to play in the most unscrupulous manner'. Those who ascended the *altiplanos* with Pizarro hunted down the Incas with bloodhounds, just for the sport of it. They pillaged palaces and temples, tortured and murdered to obtain gold for their king. They were eminently successful. Soon great treasure fleets were carrying back thousands of ounces of Peruvian gold every year across the Atlantic to Spain.

In the hope of obtaining gold men have voluntarily undertaken feats of superhuman endurance. In 1849 gold fever drove 50,000 men across the breadth of the United States to dig for gold on the banks of the Feather River at the foot of the Sierra Nevada. The great 100-day trek began one April night, when thousands of wagons assembled on the Missouri borders. One man, who watched its start, described the scene in these words: 'On every side as far as you can see tonight', he wrote, 'earthly stars twinkle on the ground, the camp fires of the most excited army that has ever assembled in the New World . . . No earlier cause ever called together such a strange medley of men, so curious a mass as this Golden Army – rich men, poor men, beggar men, thieves . . . all dreaming of gold here where the California trails zig-zag away over a hundred rough knolls.' They little knew, this army, what they faced. They were thinking of gold, not of the 'starvation and cholera and hard work and slaughter'. In Nevada, in an area of 15 square miles, 362 wagons were later found abandoned together with the bones of 350 horses, 280 oxen and 120 mules. Miraculously, 40,000 of the original 50,000 men got through. Some of them even found gold. By 1851 the forty-niners and those who had joined them at the diggings – having crossed the seas from Australia and China and Europe – were taking $2\frac{1}{2}$ million ounces of alluvial gold out of the gravels in the Sacramento Valley. Those men were pursuing the security gold can afford. Some of them found it. More often – and even to the successful – the 'security' proved an illusion, as it has done at other periods of history.

After Scipio Africanus had defeated the Carthaginians, at the beginning of the 2nd century B.C., Rome gained access to the rich gold deposits of Spain. This ushered in a new age of opulence. Magnificent gold coins were struck, and the guild of goldsmiths in Rome was flooded with orders for gold jewellery and plate from the Imperial and noble families of the city. This Spanish gold, the vast hoard which Trajan's conquest of Dacia made available, and gold booty which Augustus brought back from Egypt, gave the Romans enormous purchasing power in the market places of the world. With it they could buy gems from India, silks from China, furs from Russia. But was gold really such a boon to the Romans? It is often contended that the gold and the luxuries it bought ultimately created the very reverse of security – undermining the Roman character and contributing to Rome's decline and fall.

Besides purchasing luxuries, gold fulfilled another function for the Romans: it provided them with a means of pacifying the enemies at the gates of their great Empire. 'It is impossible', C. H. V. Sutherland wrote, 'to guess the quantity of gold drained off in the form of subsidies to conciliate the barbarian nations just across the frontiers.' The gold medallions with which Rome 'bought' peaceful neighbours, have been found in Germany, in Romania, in Yugoslavia and in Hungary.

Eventually, however, so many were Rome's commitments that the demand for gold exceeded the supply and the barbarians fell upon the weakened Empire. Before this happened the Roman economy had become hopelessly over-extended and the citizens of Rome were burdened with taxes in an endeavour to maintain the subsidies. This is a situation with which we ourselves are all too familiar; gold seems to exist not for our pleasure, but as a yoke we must bear. Lord Keynes described gold as a barbarous relic, and in recent years a number of economists have suggested that the world would be a better place to live in if we could rid ourselves of this golden burden. Unfortunately no one has yet devised an acceptable alternative, and the governments of the leading nations of the world continue to regard gold as the ultimate international 'reserve asset'.

Only to the craftsmen who have worked in the metal through the centuries has gold invariably remained the 'perfect' element that it was considered at the dawn of civilisation. Gold is the supreme raw material, so workable because of its great malleability and ductility, so beautiful because of its colour and brilliance, so permanent because of its nobility, so adaptable because of its suitability for every type of artefact that its possibilities seem infinite.

The beautiful objects which craftsmen have fashioned from gold are the main concern of this book, but art, particularly golden art, cannot be studied in a vacuum. Goldsmiths cannot flourish unless they have plenty of gold on which to work. This, sadly, has not always been the case. Often the goldsmith has had to depend for his supplies upon the fortitude of an army and the brilliance of its general to conquer gold-bearing territories. Such campaigns have not invariably been successful, while defeats have frequently worsened the goldsmith's position – forcing the king who launched the venture to use the gold in his treasury to hire mercenaries to defend his country's boundaries, rather than commission the goldsmith to make use of it in his art.

The goldsmiths, besides being subject to the abilities of generals, the fortitude of armies, the whims of kings, and the expediencies of politics, have also depended upon the skill and good fortune of prospectors. Gold has always been a rare commodity. All man's efforts to discover gold have won from the earth not more than 60,000 to 70,000 tons of it, and most of this has been mined in the past hundred years. The history of goldsmithing has therefore been sporadic. In the early days the ancient Greeks, for instance, had little gold and therefore few goldsmiths. Later the finds in Thrace, and the conquests of Alexander the Great, resulted in a flourishing craft and the smiths of Greece gained international fame. The history of goldsmithing in Rome followed a similar pattern, until eventually the invading barbarians, temporarily at least, extinguished the fires in the workshops. War, when it has not opened up new supplies of precious metals, has often robbed the goldsmith of his raw material and of the patronage upon which he depends. In the aftermath of war all is austerity. The skilled labour has been dispersed and must be slowly re-recruited. Only gradually do men's minds turn again to the gracious things of life, some of which the goldsmith can provide.

New gold finds have always been a great stimulus to the goldsmith's craft. The Spanish conquests in South and Central America resulted in a great age of goldsmithing in Renaissance Europe. The discovery of previously untapped resources of alluvial gold in the Urals in the 19th century led to the lavish use of gold by the Tsars and by the Russian Orthodox Church. The gold rushes in California, in the Klondike and in Australia in the same century, resulted in a greater use of gold for personal adornment than had ever been possible before. As wealth became more widely distributed following the Industrial Revolution, more people aspired to wear gold. The metal was available, and goldsmithing was industrialised to supply the demand. In America and in Europe thousands of girls stamped out the components of brooches, lockets and ear-rings on fly-presses. Dramatic stories from the goldfields made headlines in the world's newspapers. Everyone talked about gold; everyone wanted gold.

In the 20th century more gold has been won from the earth than at any time in history. In 1966 alone 41,700,000 ounces were recovered in the non-Communist world. Of this total, 74 per cent (nearly 31,000,000 ounces) came from the giant Witwatersrand Reef in South Africa. This quartz reef was first discovered in 1886, but because of its size and the depth to which shafts have to be sunk to reach the gold-bearing conglomerate, half a century and a vast capital investment were needed to exploit it fully. Since 1886 this reef has yielded over 800,000,000 ounces of gold, a third of all the gold that man has recovered during 6,000 years.

When one remembers that, at its height, the California gold rush yielded only 3 million ounces a year, one would imagine that today's production would be more than adequate for the craftsmen's needs. Indeed today gold wares are produced on a scale never before approached. In thousands of jewellers' windows in towns and cities throughout the world, gold watches and gold rings, gold bracelets and gold brooches are displayed. Anyone with a little money can aspire to gold ownership, for gold is no longer the exclusive prerogative of the wealthy.

Despite this relative profusion, however, there is still not enough gold to go around. The gold reserves of a great nation can be drained overnight by a handful of currency speculators, and the goldsmith can find himself proscribed in the national interest. Goldwares are heavily taxed in many countries. In Britain in 1970 for example, the goldsmith's wares were loaded with a 55 per cent purchase tax to discourage the public from buying them.

In Britain and America people are prohibited from owning gold bullion. Behind such prohibitions lies the fact that gold has acquired a new importance for the individual. In an age of economic uncertainty and of general inflation, people have lost faith in currencies. They buy gold as a hedge, because every year their money purchases fewer goods.

The vast scale of private gold hoarding today was revealed by Timothy Green in his book *The World of Gold*. 'In 1965', he wrote,' of the $2 billion coming onto the market, the private hoarder snapped up over $1¼ billion, leaving a scant $240 million for official monetary reserves after industry and the arts had claimed their $500 million . . . The total value of gold in private hands at the end of 1967 was estimated to be over $20 billion.'

Of the share of the gold which is available annually to industry and the arts, industry is absorbing an increasing percentage at the expense of the artists – the goldsmiths. Miniature electronic circuits are being produced in ever increasing numbers, for everything from transistorised radios to computers. Gold, because of its corrosion resistance, has proved to be the ideal contact material, and so the electronics industry is prepared to buy gold at any price. The textile industry too is in the market for gold. Again, because of gold's nobility, it is needed for the spinnerets used in the production of synthetic fibres. The American space programme has found gold essential as a high-energy cosmic radiation shield on capsules. Such industrial uses are certain to increase, and so the goldsmith has three powerful competitors for the available gold – governments, private speculators and industry. As the goldsmith still remains a relatively small operator his livelihood could be threatened, even in an age when more gold is being taken out of the ground each year than was recovered in a century in the past.

One problem which faces anyone who sets out to compile a book about the arts of the goldsmith is the fact that gold wares, despite their potential permanence, tend to disappear within a relatively short time after they have been made. Even the gold which was consigned to the pyramids and was supposed to surround the dead Egyptian kings forever, had mostly been spirited away long before the first archaeologist penetrated the burial chambers. By 1800 B.C. robbers had pillaged virtually every tomb in the Valley of the Kings at Luxor. The temptations which faced these robbers were considerable, as the finds made in the tomb of Tutankhamun in 1922 demonstrated. The innermost coffin alone would have repaid any effort, or any risk, a robber might have been involved in. It was made entirely of gold which was between 2½ and 3 millimetres thick. Even in more modern times goldwares have had a habit of disappearing. A king, like Charles I, in debt in the middle of a long war, would melt down the painstaking work of a hundred goldsmiths without compunction. Fashion too is an enemy of the art historian. People are not so sentimental about heirlooms as they are supposed to be.

Kings, in common with those whom they ruled, have by and large shown little interest in the products of a past age. Anything, from royal regalia to the simplest ring, is likely to be remodelled by those who inherit it.

From what has been said, it can be seen that gold has been an all-pervading influence on the history of mankind. It has given total power to some, brought abject misery to others, among them those tens of thousands of men, women and children who have been forced to slave all their lives in dark tunnels to win a few ounces of yellow metal from the soil. Greed for gold has both destroyed civilisations and laid the foundations of such important new industrial nations as South Africa and Australia.

Small wonder that gold has such a hold on our imagination! Yet all these overtones sometimes obscure the simple fact that gold is a beautiful metal, a superb raw material in the hands of a great craftsman. In the course of history some of the most magnificent objects which man has created have been wrought in gold. In our own time jewellers continue to work in a tradition that reaches back 8,000 years or more – using gold in new ways, giving it new forms, creating, as the goldsmith has always done, objects of great beauty as well as great value, perpetuating a major art form.

Part One

1
The World in Search of Gold

Gold exists all around us, in the ground, in the waters of rivers, in the sea, in plants, and even in our own bodies. Yet it remains tantalisingly difficult to extract in worthwhile quantities. In the past five centuries we have managed to obtain probably no more than 50,000 tons of it. Melted down and cast into a single cube, this would measure only 15 yards by 15 yards by 15 yards.

Gold was created during the infancy of our planet, when from the great inner cauldron flaming jets of gas and liquid burst through the thin outer crust into a turbulent landscape where innumerable volcanos were erupting and new-born mountain ranges cooled in the atmosphere.

In the cooling process the volcanic rock solidified, and some of the fluids from below squirted into its fissures and channels, spreading like veins below the skin of the globe. As the fury died out of the invading currents chemical reactions took place between some of the gases and liquids and the rock itself, and out of the resulting solutions many strange and beautiful substances crystallised. Among them were gemstones and gold.

The classic gold crystal takes the same form as the classic diamond crystal, that of an octahedron. But there are many variants, making gold as fascinating to the crystallographer as it is to the craftsman or the collector. The crystals are normally found in complex clusters, some resembling leaves, some like skeins of glittering wire, others like abstract sculpture twined round a matrix of quartz.

No treasure hunt is complete without a sprinkling of false and misleading clues, and nature has a couple to taunt the prospector. One of them is to arrange that gold is most often found in quartz, one of the commonest of all minerals. Gold is also found in deposits of sulphides, particularly in association with iron pyrites. This is the stuff which deluded so many inexpert prospectors that it bears the name of 'Fool's Gold'.

Two 15th-century illustrations showing, left, *the use of the rocker to separate gold from the alluvia in which it was found and,* right, *shaft mining in alluvial deposits. From Agricola's* De Re Metallica.

Right: *typical late Etruscan work – a huge repoussé ear-ring from the 3rd or 4th century* B.C. *British Museum.*

Science recognises gold as an element, a substance which resists analysis. So far nobody has contrived a formula to manufacture it, though that has not been for want of trying. To this king of metals, chemistry gives the symbol *Au*. It is non-ferrous, and considerably heavier than lead. It has an atomic weight of 196.967 and a specific gravity of 19.32. It has a fairly low melting point of 1,063° centigrade and it boils at 2,660° centigrade, a little higher than recent estimates of the temperature in the earth's mantle.

Gold is remarkable both for its physical properties and for the way these combine to produce its wonderful versatility. It is at once the most malleable and the most ductile of metals, and after silver is is the most reflective. Its malleability makes it very easy to work. A skilled craftsman can hammer it out into foil 0.00005 in thick, and an ounce of it will yield a sheet 100 ft square. Gold sheet was used by furniture makers as veneers, and by artists as enrichments on triptychs and manuscripts. The ductility enables an ounce of gold to be drawn through dies until it gives a mile of wire the diameter of a hair. Jewellers of many periods have exploited this quality to produce the finest chains and subtle webs of filigree.

Its great reflectivity is the secret of the brightness of this metal; and the quality called 'nobility' is what keeps this brightness from fading. To describe a metal as noble is not merely a poet's whimsy. Technically, it means one that is not attacked by oxygen, neither rusting like iron nor corroding like copper. Furthermore it is impervious to most acids. For this reason, gold has proved to be a boon to modern industry. Where life and efficiency depend on the sure functioning of tiny contacts, whether in hospital equipment or in today's space-vehicles, there gold is used. The same nobility which commended it to the rulers of the ancient world now helps to widen the boundaries of our own.

It was not man who sought gold at the outset, but nature that brought it to him. For thousands of centuries it lay hidden inside the hills. Gradually wind, rain and snow eroded the rock of the outcrops until the crystals were freed from its grip. With the other débris, the gold was tumbled down from high places by the winter torrents, and glaciers carried it slowly into the valleys below.

Left, above: *the gold inner coffin from the 18th-dynasty tomb of Tutankhamun, showing the sculptural mastery of the Egyptian goldsmith. Cairo Museum. Below: hair ornament in the form of a lion griffon from the Oxus treasure. Inset: Lydian gold stater, issued between 560 and 546 B.C., the first gold coin ever made. The impression shows facing heads of a lion and a bull. British Museum.*

When it reached the flat land, it sank to the beds of the streams because of its heaviness, often to be covered by layer upon layer of alluvial deposits. Here and there, crystals came together and compounded, forming the little gold pebbles we call nuggets. The currents of the streams rounded and polished them (as jewellery is still polished by tumbling it with stones and water). When the streams were clear and the sun shone, the nuggets on the bottom glittered, and where the streams no longer ran they gleamed out of the dried-up beds. They lay there while life formed on earth until finally men lifted them up and made them sacred.

Gold in sufficient quantity to merit extraction has been found in the Middle and Far East, in the Urals of Russia, in North and South America, in Africa and Australia, and in many parts of Europe. Man has laboriously panned the rivers of the world, scrabbled out primitive tunnels, chiselled shafts and blasted galleries into quartz reefs to reach buried deposits.

Most of the earliest gold mines were alluvial workings, for these required neither great skill nor much equipment. The shabby prospector with his shovel and pan, and his grubstake loaded on a *burro*, is a central character of the gold legend; all he needs to make his fortune is luck and a supply of water. Having found what from experience or superstition he believes to be a likely area, he loads his flat metal pan with a shovelful of grit, sand and pebbles and adds water to it. Then he twirls and tilts the pan, washing away the mixture little by little. If there is any gold, its weight will make it sink to the base of the pan, to be revealed as a few glinting grains or pea-sized nuggets.

Alluvial gold is sometimes called 'placer' gold, from the Spanish-American word for deposit. Much of it, however, is in the form of dust. In Mexico, Peru and Asia sand and gravel were washed over rough fabric, sheepskins or goatskins, and the heavy gold grains were trapped on the textured surface or in the greasy hairs. This is probably the basis of the legend of the Golden Fleece, for which Jason and the Argonauts searched on the Black Sea coast.

Once a prospector established that a find was worth working, he began to mechanise his operations. He set up a rocker, a sloping wooden trough above which is a cradle that can be rocked back and forth. A rocker system in a 15th-century European mine is illustrated in Agricola's *De Re Metallica*, but the device may have been invented thousands of years earlier.

The drawing shows a sophisticated production line. Rockers hang above a long trough with little tables at intervals along it. The cradles have handles to facilitate the rocking, and holes in their bases show that they act as sieves, each finer than the last. The alluvium was tipped into a chute at the top end of the line and washed along from table to table, to be sieved and graded. At the bottom, three more workers shake fine sieves over butts of water to catch any fugitive specks that may have got past the tables. In 19th-century

A 16th-century illustration showing Appalachian Indians dredging the bed of a stream for gold using hollow sticks.

---

cradles a rocking cam was substituted for the handle, and the trough had a canvas base. The canvas was stretched over so-called 'rifle bars' and any gold left by the washing was caught in the pouch-like depressions formed between them. The cradle, crude though it looks, was a very efficient piece of extraction machinery.

The effort to win gold has always sharpened man's observation of physics and logic, even in the simplest societies. A drawing of about 1560 shows

Appalachian Indians pushing hollow sticks into the bed of a stream and shaking the plug of sand out on the bank. This process is the forerunner of the dredgers whose clanking still echoes along the Klondike as they scoop out the river bottom and spew the tailings ashore.

As people learned more about gold and its sources, they realised that picking through a stream and then moving on was a shortsighted endeavour. What lay on the top might be only a hint of riches buried below, for in many places lush alluvial beds had been overlaid with later and scantier deposits.

Detail from a contemporary drawing which illustrates gold mining in California in the last century. Bibliothéque National, Paris.

Anyone with the initiative to dig through the surface silt might be well rewarded.

Panning was easy enough, a one-man activity. But delving on this scale required industrial organisation and specialist workers. Shafts had to be sunk in the wilderness, galleries propped up, hoists erected to bring up the gravels, water piped to the head of the shaft, complex washing rigs assembled. The early installations must have looked as strange as a modern nuclear plant in a desert. And there were casualties. Tunnels collapsed, and there was always the danger of flooding. In the north, before they could dig at all, they had to soften the permafrost by building fires. This was how they won the gold in the Yukon, inching their way down through the overburden, using fire and spade alternatively.

There is one other way to wring gold from alluvial deposits. This is hydraulic mining, which the Romans employed in Spain. Writing in the 1st century A.D., Strabo described how 'they led water to the arid spots to make the gold dust glitter'. A powerful jet of water was directed at a sloping site to remove the surface alluvia and expose the gold. The ground was then picked over by hand.

But gold is not won only from alluvia, it is also recovered from the mother lodes. The gold-bearing rock is hacked out, then crushed to powder, so that the gold can be separated from it. All this requires a large and organised labour force. The evidence points to the Egyptians as the first people to extract gold from a quartz reef. Their kings could do this only because they had an endless supply of slave miners. Diodorus, writing in the 2nd century B.C., described conditions in the hill mines along the Red Sea between Berenice and Coptos, where galleries up to four miles long had been hewn out. What he saw had been going on for thousands of years.

'The king of Egypt', he wrote, 'consigned to the gold mines those who had been condemned for crimes and who had been made captive in war . . . many in number and all bound with fetters.' Often, it seems, their families were sent with them. These hapless legions of men, women, and children had to break down the reef by cracking the quartz with fire and chisels. Those strong enough 'cut the glimmering rock with iron pickaxes . . . and they hew out the galleries, not following a straight course, but according to the vein'. Boys collected the broken quartz and carried it out to the surface workers. In the open, men 'pounded the quartz in stone mortars with iron pestles'. The women, and men too old for heavier work, fed it into mills which ground it 'as fine as wheat flour'. The powdered ore was spread on sloping boards over which water was continually poured, and thus the gold was recovered.

Much has been written of the toiling armies who built the pyramids. The effort of the prisoners who burrowed out these mines was comparable in scale, but it has generally gone unregarded. The old workings, opened perhaps as early as 3000 B.C., are still to be seen. Tailings found at one site suggest that in this mine alone a million tons of quartz was removed to get at the gold. By 2000 B.C., it has been calculated, 1,500,000 lb of gold was extracted from the Red Sea reefs, and when Julius Caesar arrived in Egypt in 43 B.C. they were still yielding.

Why were the Pharaohs so gluttonous for gold? Why, long before them, did the early settlers in Upper Egypt bother to collect a metal too soft to make a good hoe or axe, too heavy to make a useful food-pot? To an agricultural people the sun is all-important, and gold was the thing on earth which most closely resembled the sun. The tribes of the Nile Valley, who worshipped animals and trees and rocks, had more than 2,000 gods all told. But the sun god Ra became their supreme deity, and the people believed the Egyptian kings were his sons. Gold was used in the sun-worship rituals, and from being associated with the kings and priests it was next proclaimed to be their prerogative. In life, it was part of the regal panoply that set the king apart from his subjects. He sat on a golden throne, wearing a golden head-dress and a golden collar and sandals, gleaming like the sun itself. In death, which the Egyptians regarded as simply an extension of their existence, he was surrounded by the many golden articles he would need with him in his after life. There was no fear that these might crumble with the passing of years or lose their splendour.

The graves found in the valley of the Euphrates show that the Babylonians, who were Egypt's neighbours to the east, were equally enamoured of golden trappings. It was inevitable that, as the Egyptians widened their obsessive search for gold to other regions, it would be recognised abroad as a valuable commodity. They were importing gold from Nubia ('nub' was the Egyptian word for gold) as well as Ethiopia. By the 14th century B.C. they were exporting it to Babylon, Syria and Assyria. Tushratta, the Mittanian king whose sister had married Amenophis III of Egypt, wrote, 'Send me much gold, more gold, for in my brother's land gold is as common as dust.' The king of Babylon was a man of few words: 'If during this harvest you send the gold concerning which I wrote to you, then I will give you my daughter.' But when he received only two pounds of gold he complained of the Egyptian ruler's lack of generosity. The Egyptians probably also paid in gold for the products of Mycenae and for Minoan pottery from Crete.

As the demand for gold spread, so did the practice of tomb-robbing. Although the architects tried to foil the robbers by concealing the royal burial chambers, scarcely a single tomb was not 'robbed in antiquity'. A papyrus document of the 12th Dynasty (2000–1700 B.C.) records the confession of one Amenpnufer, a light-fingered stonemason who used his copper tools to break into the pyramid of Sekhemra Shedtaui with seven

A pectoral from the tomb of Tutankhamun. Cairo Museum.

accomplices. Opening the sarcophagi of the king and queen, they found the late monarch 'equipped with a falchion, a large number of amulets and jewels of gold . . . the noble mummy of this king was completely bedecked with gold, and his coffins were adorned with gold'. They divided the spoils and crossed over to Thebes, where Amenpnufer was imprisoned in the mayor's office. He bribed his way out with his slave and rejoined his companions, who compensated him for his loss, and they returned to their trade of robbery.

In a country where gold was under royal control, one wonders how they disposed of the loot. But there were certainly ready markets for it, including foreign merchants and treasuries. And as first the Persians, and later the Romans, descended on Egypt as conquerors, the gold of the Pharaohs was dispersed among these emergent powers.

Persia was the second great gold centre of the ancient world. Militarily, in the 5th century B.C. she represented doom to Babylon and all the old nations. Belshazzar, feasting in his palace from the gold vessels which his father Nebuchadnezzar had stolen from the Temple of Jerusalem, was apparently oblivious of the enemy at the gates. Quickly overwhelming his kingdom, the Persians swept on until their empire extended from the Black Sea to the eastern Mediterranean and across to India.

When Darius I sat in state to receive tribute in his new city of Persepolis, representatives of 29 subjugated nations filed past. He had access to all the major gold areas then known, except those in Spain, which the Phoenicians controlled. One of the most important was the state of Lydia, ruled by King Croesus.

The legendary source of the riches of Croesus was the alluvial deposits of the River Pactolus. He was the first king to mint gold coins. The Egyptians had issued standard gold rings which were used as money, and Croesus's predecessor, Ardys, had introduced Lydian coins made of electrum, a natural alloy of gold and silver. In about 500 B.C. Croesus minted the famous gold coins stamped with his insignia, the facing heads of a lion and a bull.

By doing so, he had taken two far-reaching steps. First, by guaranteeing the coins with his insignia he had produced a medium of exchange that everyone would accept. Secondly, he had democratised gold. Though many countries might continue to restrict the wearing of it to the courts, nobles and priests, from this time forward any diligent merchant could amass coins. Eventually this was to create a new profession, banking, and bankers were often to assume as much importance in deciding the fate of nations as the kings they served.

In an effort to decide the fate of his country, Croesus consulted the Oracle at Delphi. At that time the Persians were still threatening Lydia. If he were to go to war against them would he be successful? As an offering, he sent to the shrine of Apollo a quantity of gold which C. H. V. Sutherland suggests was no less than 7,500 lb. The Oracle informed him that if he took up arms 'a great king would be overthrown'. He assumed this meant Cyrus, the Persian ruler of the day. But it was the Lydians who were defeated in battle, and King Croesus threw himself on his own funeral pyre. He had paid heavily for the Oracle's double-edged counsel.

The Persians, despite their enormous wealth, military skill and administrative ability, had a relatively short period of glory before the Greeks challenged and overthrew them. The Athenians were so poor that they frequently took golden statues and offerings from their temples to pay for their campaigns – restoring good relations with the gods afterwards as they captured more and more of the Persians' hoards.

After the battle of Plataea, the Spartan general showed his officers the golden cups and bowls from the royal baggage train he had seized. 'I desire to show you the foolishness of the leader of the Medes', said Pausanias. 'With such provision for life as you see, they came here to take away from us ours which is so humble.'

The critical conflict in the war was the naval battle of Salamis in 480 B.C., when a Greek fleet, paid for in silver, routed a Persian one built with gold. All the citizens of Athens were shareholders in the silver mines at Laurium, to the north of the city. When a rich new vein was discovered there, Themistocles persuaded them to plough their profits into additional fighting

An elaborate Greek ear-ring made in the 4th century B.C., *with stylised flowers, pendant figures and skilled granulation. Schmuckmuseum, Pforzheim.*

galleys. Greece was well rewarded for this sacrifice. After the final defeat of the Persians by Alexander the Great, vast hoards of gold flowed into Greece. For the first time goldsmiths in a European culture could express themselves without restraint. They were to produce some of the most beautiful gold jewellery the world has ever seen, and for hundreds of years they were to influence the goldcraft of the Mediterranean area, the new centre of power of the pre-Christian world.

Alexander was not only a brilliant general. He was a wise statesman, and he knew the power of gold in statecraft. On his eastern march of conquest he had a gold prospector on his staff.

Meanwhile three new civilisations were springing up at the western end of the Mediterranean – the Etruscans, the Carthaginians and the Romans. The Etruscans, who established themselves in Italy, were excellent goldsmiths, and their work had a most distinctive style. Possibly they obtained their gold from the rivers that ran down the Alps and formed the Po; or they may have brought it from Spain. Already by this time the Phoenicians were tapping the rich mineral resources in the valley of the Guadalquivir, and they had long been developing their thriving port of trade at Cadiz, opposite the great Phoenician city of Carthage in North Africa.

Herodotus described the taciturn routine of Carthaginian sailors for collecting gold on their coastal forays:

They come here and unload their cargo; then having laid it orderly by the waterline, they go aboard their ships and light a smoking fire. The people of the country see the smoke, and coming to the shore they lay down gold to pay for the cargo and withdraw away from the wares. Then the Carthaginians disembark and examine the gold; if it seems to them a fair price for their cargo they take it and go their ways; but if not, they go aboard again and wait, and the people come back and add more gold until the shipmen are satisfied . . . the Carthaginians do not lay hands on the gold until it matches the value of their cargo, nor do the people touch the cargo till the shipmen have taken the gold.

Neither Carthage nor Rome were to produce spectacular artefacts in gold. The Carthaginians were copyists rather than innovators, making provincial imitations of Egyptian and Greek models, and the Romans revered gold more for its purchasing power than for its beauty.

The mighty Roman civilisation grew from a poor city-state founded about 800 B.C. It was not until five centuries later, when the 28-year-old Scipio Africanus finally defeated Carthage with his victory over Hannibal, that Rome at last had access to gold in any quantity. As the Romans pushed deeper into Spain, they combed the deposits with typical thoroughness. Strabo wrote of rivers and torrents carrying down 'the golden sand . . .

nuggets of up to half a pound in weight'. Pliny reported lumps retrieved from the sediment of rivers like the Tagus, 'purer than any other gold and polished by attrition in the running stream'. Roman reef mining 'may seem to surpass the achievement of the giants. For by the light of lanterns mountains are hollowed out.' When the miners encountered flint they broke it up 'by using fire and then vinegar' or with heavy iron rams.

Gold from the empire allowed Rome to import luxuries from all over the known world; but, as Gibbon claimed, 'prosperity ripened the principle of decay'. By the 3rd century B.C., a succession of self-indulgent emperors and periodic civil wars had weakened the genius of this civilisation, and the barbarians from the north were gathering on its borders. Roman gold, which had been used to produce beautiful coins and rather uninspired jewellery and plate, was offered in ingots in an effort to placate them. But this did not delay the destruction for very long. In 410 the Visigoths sacked Rome itself, after they had twice been bought off with bribes of gold – and, interestingly, pepper. The Vandals sacked it again in 455, and in 476 the Roman empire collapsed entirely.

The 'dark ages' that followed were not the cultural abyss they were once represented to be. The peoples of the north had been building up a gold culture of their own for a thousand years before they swept down on Rome. That city, with Milan, remained an important centre of goldsmithing for at least two more centuries, during which a glorious golden door was made for the Basilica of the Vatican, and a host of other rich embellishments for the new Christian churches.

With Europe in turmoil and administration in ruins, the Church was to be the main focus of culture in Europe for the next 500 years. Not only did it provide patronage, but skills and learning were kept alive within the monastery walls. Theophilus in his *Diversarum Artium Schedula* says: 'Monasteries are built so that the various arts may be practised.' They were equipped with 'furnaces, bellows, anvils, tanks, and the organarium for drawing the gold out into threads'. The monasteries at St Albans and Ely were leading centres of clerical goldsmithing in England, and Saint Eligius was a goldsmith in the Merovingian court in France. Charlemagne created another centre at Aachen, importing Byzantine smiths to work 16 cartloads of precious metals he had captured from the Avars, as well as gifts of Arab treasure from the Caliph of Baghdad.

The churches of Byzantium, like the great Hagia Sophia, glittered with gold. Golden altars, doors, lamps, crosses, chalices, reliquaries and gospel covers poured out of the workshops. The Empress Theodora, reigning in 856, possessed 109,000 lb of gold. Gold came to Constantinople both by trade and conquest, and it went out again in glorious golden coins from the imperial mint, which bought furs from Russia, carpets from Persia and jewels and spices from India. But Byzantium declined as Islam rose, and Mohammed's armies, united by the Koran, overran North Africa, the Middle East and large areas of Europe.

The Arabs, like the Phoenicians, were more concerned to use gold in the development of trade than for adornment; and apart from some goldwares chased all over with the patterns of leaves and flowers known as arabesques, the zenith of Islam was not a notable age for goldwork. Nevertheless, the Arabs ranged far to accumulate it. From Timbuktu, the 'city of gold' on the Niger, the yellow dust was carried on camel-back 2,000 miles across the Sahara. In the 10th century Islam's gold stocks dwindled as the Crusaders piously transported their captures to their homelands.

From this time forward, there was increased mining activity in Europe. Mines were opened up in the Alps, in Bohemia and Siberia, and Hungary became the principal European source of gold. The Portuguese in West Africa tapped the mines of what came to be called the Gold Coast. With this influx, a great upsurge in production of goldwares began in the medieval workshops, and imaginative jewellery of a new delicacy emerged. The smiths grouped themselves into powerful guilds and looked forward to rich profits.

Unfortunately one war followed another in quick succession, and with the invention of artillery the cost of waging war had risen steeply. Often the goldsmiths were neglected while the armourers thrived. When Henry V took his small army to France in 1415 he had to pay 13 shillings and fourpence a day for a duke, four shillings for a baron, two for a knight and sixpence for an archer. He had 75 gunners, 120 miners, with specialist and support forces ranging from tentmakers to chaplains and clerks. And, although the City of London lent him £32,000 and the church £9,000, Henry had to pawn his crown jewels to finance the venture.

A new zenith in the history of gold came after Columbus discovered the New World in 1492. Cortés in Mexico and Pizarro in Peru came upon two civilisations immensely rich in gold, and in their eagerness to acquire it they destroyed both of them. The Aztec and Inca alike seem to have accepted the inevitability of a fate prophesied by 'our father the sun . . . that unknown people would arrive, that they would obtain victory and subjugate all our kingdom'. They offered little resistance to the determined handful of Spanish freebooters. And the deluge of gold that poured home in the treasure fleets, with the galleons labouring low in the water under the weight of their glittering cargo, helped to transform Europe into the rich and forceful area it became in the 17th, 18th and 19th centuries.

The Aztecs called gold 'the sweat of the sun' and allowed it to be worn only by royalty and nobility. They fashioned discs from it which had magic significance, and the dependent tribes paid tribute in gold to the emperor,

Moctezuma. He was also head priest of their cruel religion, in which queues of men, women and children waited on the steps of their temples to have their hearts torn out. Bernal Diaz recorded that at the great temple of Tezcatlipoca the effigy of the chief god 'was made of all kinds of seeds, which had been ground and kneaded with the blood of virgin boys and girls . . . At the time of their feasts they adorned the figure with the kind of gold jewellery they wore when they dressed for great festivals.'

What these gods had decreed, Moctezuma could not alter; and after only a few skirmishes he allowed the Spaniards to walk into his capital, Tenochtitlán, and take him prisoner. It took three days to share out the gold in his treasure rooms among the 580 men of the column of *conquistadores*. In today's money, this hoard was worth about £3,000,000 or $7,200,000. Cortés took a third for himself and put aside the fifth reserved for the King of Spain. His men divided the rest.

But some of the Aztec leaders were less inclined to accept the gloomy judgment of the gods, and they resented their emperor's collaboration with the gold-hungry invaders. Moctezuma was injured in an Aztec revolt, and the Spaniards left him dead as they retreated from the city. Tenochtitlán was built in the middle of a lake, and many men died as they tried to fight a rear-guard action along the narrow causeways, encumbered by the gold they refused to relinquish. Cortés reached the shore, assembled a new army of 900 Spaniards and 90,000 Indian mercenaries and attacked the capital. In 90 days of fighting, 50,000 Aztecs were massacred and the lake city was reduced to ruins. The defiant Cuauhtémoc, who had taken over as emperor and organised the resistance, was 'put to the fire'.

The gold lost in the retreat had been thrown into the lake, but the whole country was systematically pillaged as it was subdued. Cortés had access to the alluvial workings in the Mixtec provinces in the south: so rich are these deposits that Mexico even today recovers 200,000 ounces of gold yearly.

While Cortés was settling his newly conquered realm, his countryman Francisco Pizarro was discovering gold in South America. He put landing parties ashore in Peru at the bay of Túmbez in 1526. They returned with tales of incredible splendours of gold and silver and 'virgins of the sun'. Pizarro could neither read nor write but he could calculate an opportunity. Before making his try for this treasure, he wanted to make sure that he should keep more of it than anyone else. He withdrew to Spain and returned with the appointment of Captain-General of the lands he planned to conquer. In 1531 he landed in Peru with 180 men.

Pizarro was in luck. The old Inca emperor had died and his two sons were fighting a civil war over the succession. In the aftermath, Pizarro easily recruited Indian auxiliaries, then pushed 9,000 ft up the misty defiles of the Andes to confront the new king, Atahualpa. When he reached Cajamarca on

33

the central plateau there was a half-hour battle in which nearly 6,000 Indians were butchered and Atahualpa himself captured. The conquest of Peru was virtually over.

The Spaniards were accompanied by friars and bibles. But Atahualpa soon observed 'amidst all the show of religious zeal in his conquerors, a lurking appetite more potent . . . a love of gold'. Playing on their cupidity, he told them that if they freed him he would have a room 17 ft by 22 ft filled with gold, and two similar ones with silver. Pizarro accepted, and messengers began to bring in the ransom. 'History affords no parallel of such a booty', Prescott wrote in *The Conquest of Peru*. In modern terms, there were some £14,000,000, or $33,600,000, to be divided among Pizarro's small force. There were goblets, ewers, temple ornaments, wonderful animal sculptures, a superbly worked representation of Indian corn with the golden ear sheathed in broad leaves of silver, an elegant fountain which sent up a sparkling jet of gold.

The soldiers were little impressed. Gold in ingots was easier to share. Working day and night, the job of melting down the Inca goldsmiths' marvels and recasting them took no less than a month. When it was over, Atahualpa was tried on, among other charges, those of 'idolatory, and of adulterous practices'. Threatened with death by fire as a heretic, he agreed to embrace the Christian faith, and was thereupon garrotted instead. In June 1541, while dining with his captains, Pizarro himself was assassinated by a disaffected compatriot.

The Andes were to be the most important source of Europe's gold for centuries. All the Inca gold was alluvial. It came from the high streams of the *altiplano*, in particular from the valley of Curimayo northwest of Cajamarca. But, above and beyond alluvial gold, there is always the vein or system of veins from which it must have once been swept away. This is what the old prospectors meant when they dreamed of finding the 'mother lode'. Eventually the Spaniards found such lodes in the mountains. They even had the luck to find mercury on the spot, to assist extraction from the ore. The gold from Peru was shipped to Panama and carried on mules over the isthmus to the east coast, where the treasure fleets assembled for the voyage to Spain.

The arrival of these argosies had an effect, of course, on money markets in Europe, and the bankers created networks of agents in various ports to advise on their movements. The famous Fugger correspondence, conducted by the great bankers of the Holy Roman Empire, contains many such references. One message dated 12 January 1590 confides, 'Letters from Lisbon report the arrival in Seville . . . of eight millions (ducats) in gold . . . the reason why the first ships are late is that they sailed further north than usual to avoid the English ships waiting for them.'

A gold medallion issued in 1589, showing Elizabeth I surrounded by a motto which translates 'no richer circle in the world'. British Museum.

The English had their agents too. Sir Thomas Walsingham was building up a first-class secret service for Queen Elizabeth I and it provided, among other international intelligence, a great deal of Spanish information. It was learned that the treasure ships were unprotected on their voyages from Peru to Panama. Sir Francis Drake, looking for a way to surprise this fat prey, circumnavigated the globe between 1577 and 1580. Sailing through the Magellan Straits, he attacked the Spaniards on the Pacific coast and captured 20 to 30 tons of gold, silver and precious stones. Financed by Elizabeth and her courtiers, the English captains went privateering at their own risk. If Spain complained, their queen would disown them, even as the loot was being delivered up the back stairs of her palace. However, Drake's was a hero's welcome. His haul paid for defences which were later to repel the Armada, and much of England's court plate and jewellery must have been made from this stolen gold.

From the 17th century trade between nations increased, and gold was freed from many fetters. Restrictions on its wear disappeared, and it circulated freely. Goldsmiths no longer depended on court patronage, and with the spread of private wealth their craft prospered. People of quite modest means bought gold watches and snuff-boxes, etuis and chatelaines. The supply of gold was heavily augmented by Portuguese consignments from the new Minas Geraes in Brazil, and more was found in Japan. Russia entered a phase of great mining activity in 1744 with the discovery of a gold-rich quartz reef in the Urals.

In the feudal domain of the Tsars, gold was a royal prerogative, as it had been under the Pharaohs, and there too it was mined by serfs. Some alluvial mines were run by local landowners who paid a royalty, just as those who scoured the gravels of the Nile had paid royalties to the descendants of Ra. The goldwork of 19th-century St Petersburg was as magnificent as any that has ever been seen, and the greatest of its workshops was that of Carl Fabergé. He was the last of the master goldsmiths to enjoy the unlimited opportunity of working for fabulously rich kings, and the Tsars were the last of those kings to enjoy exclusively the fruits of large-scale mining. One of the richest reefs was discovered near Ekaterinburg, and it was at Ekaterinburg that the last of the Tsars and his family were slain by their revolutionary successors.

In the middle years of the 19th century a new type of miner had emerged. He was no serf, winning gold for others for little or no reward. He was his own man, and what he found he kept, to save or squander as he chose. This was the kind of man who crossed the seas and trekked overland to the gold fields of California, Australia, South Africa and the Klondike.

The big gold rushes had a mixed impact on the world of their day, for although worship of Mammon was prevalent it was also fashionable to assert that money was the root of all evil and that gold would bring misfortune upon its owners.

John Augustus Sutter was ruined by the California gold rush which brought great wealth to other men. A former officer in the Swiss army, he emigrated in 1834 to escape his creditors. Like many of the men who developed the west, he was none too scrupulous. He used trickery to get a land grant from the Mexican governor of California in return for an undertaking to found a colony. Then, recruiting immigrants and pressing the local Indians into service, he proceeded to carve his own profitable ranch out of the 50,000 acres he had been given in the fertile Sacramento valley. Where the Sacramento joined the American River, he built a fort with factories, stores and workshops to make further profits from the settlers. In 1847, with the Mexican war over and California about to become United States territory, Sutter's restless acumen worked out a new opportunity: he would erect a sawmill to sell timber to pioneers for their homes. To give him his due, he had established a stable community in this beautiful valley which attracted the new arrivals.

On 24 January 1848 his foreman carpenter, James Marshall, found traces of gold in the tail race he had built for the mill. Sutter's reaction was unenthusiastic, and he even tried to suppress the report. Inevitably it leaked out, and soon men were panning and digging along the American River. They also found gold, and the rush began.

The price of a shovel rose from 1 dollar to 10. San Francisco was deserted. Ships were left unloaded as their crews made for the diggings. Men came from the eastern States, from Australia, Europe and all over the world. A great many of them, perhaps 4,000, died in the rush. Some set out for California in old vessels crowded to the gunwales, that foundered with all hands. Some died of cholera on the trails. Those who did get there built canvas townships and scrounged for food. In the first year the forty-niners took 575,000 ounces of gold out of the rivers of central California, valued at $10,000,000. By no means all of them made huge fortunes, but a man could easily take £10 worth a day from a claim, and some earned nine times that.

Over 40,000 diggers swarmed on to Sutter's property and into the neighbouring valleys, trampling crops, shovelling away his fertile soil. He tried to protect his ranch and establish his title to the gold. But his land grant did not include the mineral rights.

The city of Sacramento stands today on the site of Sutter's Fort. Its founder died in a Washington hotel room in 1880. For 10 years he had been living on a government grant of less than $5 a week. James Marshall, who first discovered the gold, fared even worse. He had staked a claim, but the newcomers jumped it. He went to law, but bribery and packed juries defeated him. When Marshall died, five years after Sutter, he was buried in a pauper's grave.

Some idea of the impact of the Californian strike on Europe is given by the increase in gold reserves between 1848 and 1852. Those of the Bank of

At the diggings there was often violence and drunkenness, as this contemporary drawing shows.

England rose from £12,800,000 to £20,000,000 and those of the Bank of France from £3,500,000 to £23,500,000.

Its impact on California itself was enormous too, bringing a great influx of population to a largely undeveloped area. In 1849 91,405 passengers from all over the world disembarked at the docks at San Francisco, and perhaps another 40,000 came overland to the diggings. During the three years from 1848 to 1851, 412,942 new people came to California. When the gold ran out many returned home, but a lot stayed on to develop the resources of the newest state in the Union.

Among the men who had joined the rush to the Sacramento were 7,000 from Australia. One of them was an unsuccessful farmer, Edward Hammond Hargreaves. He was unsuccessful again in California and sailed home on the barque *Emma* in 1850, having found nothing. He began to prospect around Bathurst in New South Wales, and in May 1851 the *Sydney Morning Herald* reported that he had struck gold at Ophir. Hargreaves was granted £10,000 and a pension for life, and his find triggered off another big rush. One strike followed another – in Queensland, in Western Australia where the Kalgoorlie mine was opened up, and in Victoria. The people of Australia went 'fossicking', and shiploads of fortune hunters arrived. A licence from the gold commissioners cost 30 shillings, and 'there were merchants, cabmen, magistrates and convicts, amateur gentlemen rocking the cradle merely to say they had done so, fashionable hairdressers and tailors, cooks, coachmen, lawyers' clerks and their masters, colliers, cobblers, quarrymen, doctors of physic and music, aldermen, an ADC on leave, scavengers, sailors, shorthand writers, a real live lord on his travels – all levelled by community of pursuit and of costume.'

Gold was a population builder. In the decade from 1851 to 1861 the population of Australia rose from 400,000 to 1,200,000. The fields there produced enormous stocks of gold, over £12,000,000 worth being taken out in 1856 in Victoria alone. Australia too produced the largest nugget of modern times, the Welcome Stranger. It measured two feet long and was found in a cart rut. The Australian fields lasted until the beginning of the 20th century, and a few prospectors had continued to find enough gold to live on until the nickel rush in our own day brought some of the ghost towns to life again.

Some years after the Australian finds, the focus of discovery shifted back to California. Some of the miners were not doing too well on the American and Feather rivers. They reasoned that if there was all this alluvial gold, there must be even greater prizes awaiting anyone who could locate the mother lodes from which it had been eroded. So some of these men began to prospect in the high country of the Sierra Nevada. In 1859 two poor Irish miners, Peter O'Riley and Pat McLaughlin, came across a reef with gold in it near what is now Virginia City in Nevada. They sold their claim to a man named Harry Comstock, who called it Comstock's Lode and sank a mine. The reef was not large, but it was immensely rich. As the Big Bonanza, this mine became America's primary source of gold for the 20 years it held out. In that period it produced $130,000,000 worth of gold and $170,000,000 of silver. Mark Twain, who was working on the Virginia City *Enterprise* at the time, recalled that 'often we felt our chairs jar, and heard the faint boom of a blast down in the bowels of the earth under the office'.

The richest gold field man has ever seen was written off as a dud by Cecil Rhodes. Diamonds had already been discovered in South Africa. The British, who had withdrawn from the territory north of the Orange River by 1854 by convention with the Boer settlers, came back in 1871 and annexed the diamond region, which had been ruled by a Griqua chief under the authority of the Orange Free State. The Boers protested vigorously, and this had much to do with their distrust of the British thereafter. Within 20 years six tons of diamonds had been mined, valued at £39,000,000. Amalgamation of various diamond groups gave the De Beers corporation, under Rhodes, a virtual monopoly of the industry.

Overshadowed by these rich diamond deposits, the South African gold industry amounted to relatively little. Gold had been found in various parts of the Transvaal, though not in any profusion, and for some years prospecting had been going on around Witwatersrand. Fred Struben, a geologist turned miner, had been extracting some gold from quartz outcrops, crushing the rock with a dolly, 'a length of timber hung from a sort of gallows on which it could be hauled up a few feet and then dropped'. But up to 1886 he and all the others working in the area probably had not recovered as much as £10,000 worth among them. In that year the great discovery was made.

There are half a dozen different versions of the great find. One of them attributes it to George Walker, who had panned for gold in Australia and was later given a pension as the original discoverer. It is now generally ascribed, however, to George Harrison, who is said to have gone walking with a frying-pan one day on land belonging to the widow Oosthuizen. As Harrison was killed by a lion afterwards he could not contest Walker's claim. At any rate, there indeed were traces of gold in these outcrops, and before long a man named J. B. Robinson turned up with £20,000 in a gladstone bag and bought seven farms totalling 40,000 acres. He had made and lost a fortune at the Kimberley diamond diggings and had persuaded another diamond man, Alfred Beit, to lend him the money against a half-share in any profits.

News of the find swept abroad, and men rushed to Africa as they had rushed to California and Australia. The usual tent and shanty town sprang up, but President Paul Kruger had put a conscientious army officer, Colonel Ferreira, in charge of it and he organised it like a military camp. Ferreira's town was the beginning of Johannesburg.

Those who came, however, found that there was no hope here for the individual fortune hunter. As more was learned about the nature of the Rand reef, it was obvious that massive amounts of capital would be required to bring out the gold. The Rand reef turned out to be nearly 300 miles long, curving beneath the earth from the far eastern Transvaal down into the Free State. H. C. Koch, chairman of Transvaal Gold Mines, has described it as a 'giant arc, resembling a huge broken saucer, bands of gold-bearing reef varying in width from a few inches thick to 15 feet, lying snugly tucked under countless millions of tons of rock'. This was why the army of hopefuls with their shovels and pans disbanded. There was nothing they could do.

The Rand gold proved to be alluvial, not native, as was at first thought. It is contained in a conglomerate of sediments which have been compacted under enormous pressure into solid rock again. The mixture is predominantly quartz, and there is less of gold in it than of anything else, just a peppering of tiny specks. The mother lode from which the gold came is believed to have been in the oldest rock formation in the world, the Swazi series formed 3,000,000,000 years ago.

How was this formidable challenge to be cracked? In the 1890s it cost no less than £500,000 to start a mine, and it was a gamble. Mining engineers predicted that the reef would peter out when the shafts got down to 25 ft. An experimental bore hole proved them wrong. It was still payable to 500 ft (later it was known to dip three miles down in places). Seven finance houses were opened in two years to provide capital for exploiting this monster. The Corner House was started by Hermann Eckstein, the Johannesburg Consolidated Investment Company by the Barnato Brothers, and Gold Fields of South Africa by Cecil Rhodes.

Deep shafts were drilled, crushing plants set up and mercury vats built to extract the gold. At first mercury extraction worked reasonably well, removing about 75 per cent of the gold from the ore. When the mines went deeper, pyrites began to appear in the ore and recovery dropped to 60 per cent – which was not enough to make the mining profitable.

Rhodes from the beginning had doubts about his Rand investment. He was dining in London in 1890 with Lord Rothschild and an American mining engineer when this depressing news arrived from South Africa. He asked the American, 'What do you do when you strike sulphide ores?' The American replied, 'Then we say, Oh God.'

It is this terse answer which is said to have persuaded Rhodes to sell his interests next morning. The value of Rand mines went down by three-quarters almost overnight. There were some 200 companies with stakes in the reef. Many sold out. Others held on and hoped. Their salvation came from Glasgow. There John MacArthur and the brothers Robert and William Forrest had been experimenting with a new extraction process, using cyanide of potassium instead of mercury. Had Rhodes' private intelligence service been as efficient as Queen Elizabeth's or that of the Fuggers, he might have heard about this in time, but he seems to have missed it completely. The three Scots came out to the Rand to demonstrate their process. In the cyanide tank the gold and its attendant impurities dissolved. The rock particles which had held it sank to the bottom. Then MacArthur and his colleagues siphoned off the solution and added zinc shavings – which precipitated the gold. Today, near the 53 mines of the Rand, you will see what look like cool green swimming pools, tempting under the hot African sun. They are tanks of potassium cyanide, which play such an important role in the extraction process.

These mines produce 30,000,000 ounces of gold a year, three-quarters of the world's supply excluding the undisclosed production of the Russian mines. South Africa, in understandable appreciation, now calls its national unit of money a rand. Had it not been for this fantastic reef, man would have had to find some new way of underpinning his currencies and balancing his trading accounts. Nor would the modern goldsmith have very much gold on which to practise his skills.

The great gold rushes were a 19th-century phenomenon, and the last of them began in 1896. George Washington Cormack was the son of a forty-niner who had crossed the great plains in a covered wagon to dig for gold. His father was still digging when he was born. When the boy grew up he shipped to Alaska as a dishwasher in a United States man-of-war, but by the time he reached Juneau he had had enough of the Navy. He jumped ship and disappeared into the wilderness. When he turned up again he was married to the daughter of a Tagish Indian chief, and he had a long drooping moustache like those worn by men of her tribe. Cormack fished for salmon where the Klondike river flows into the Yukon, south of Circle City in Canada. There were prospectors here who occasionally found gold in the creeks, and they called him Siwash George.

That summer, Siwash George was fishing in a canoe with his wife Kate, his daughter (who had the remarkable name of Graphic Gracie), and his two brothers-in-law, Skookum Jim and Tagish Charley. They met an old prospector named Henderson, who told them gold had been found in a nearby creek. They paddled off, with George dipping an old salmon tin idly into the sand now and then. At the mouth of Rabbit Creek he found a thumb-sized nugget of gold in the tin. Siwash George had come upon the richest alluvial find of all. Next day he and the two Indians staked their claims. It was 18 August 1896.

The news spread down the river and the nearby township emptied over-night. The barber from Circle City staked a claim that produced $50,000 worth of gold a year for the next five years. But it was not until two ships sailed into Seattle the following spring with three tons of gold on board that the magnitude of the strike was apparent to the outside world. *Gold, Gold, Gold, Gold* was the headline in the Seattle newspaper that day. It and others like it started 100,000 men heading for the Yukon. 'We had nothing to lose and everything to gain', Michael Macgowan, an Irish labourer working in a silver mine in Montana, wrote. It meant a chance of escaping from perpetual poverty.

Macgowan set out from Montana, then took a ship to St Michael on the

Above: *Mary's Hotel, on Bonanza Creek in the Klondike. Roadhouses sprang up along the Klondike creeks after Belinda Mulrooney opened the first one at Grand Forks in the autumn of 1898. Below: gold dust was the legal tender for almost all purchases in Dawson City during the Gold Rush. It was carried in small moosehide sacks called 'pokes'. The exchange rate was $16 an ounce. Public Archives of Canada.*

coast. Next he passed in a stern-wheeler up the 2,300-mile Yukon through a barren land. He and his companions were 'thrown out in the backwoods – not a thing to be seen but frost and snow – God alone knew the journey that lay before us'. It was October and the winter was beginning. He and other prospectors struggled through to the canvas settlement that had been dignified with the name Dawson City. Others landed from crowded, leaky ships at Skagway, Juneau and Dyea to begin the long trek inland. Many brought pack animals, most of which, Jack London wrote 'died like mosquitoes in the first frost'.

Men survived better, and some 60,000 won their way through. They climbed the Chilkoot Pass, a sheer wall of ice, weighed down by their food packs. They cut green timber at Lake Bennett and made 7,000 boats to carry them 500 miles up the Yukon to Dawson. The worst route of all was the Ashcroft trail from Edmonton through British Columbia, a 4,000-mile trek. About 1,000 men got through this way, but by the time they reached Dawson they had lost all interest in gold and set off for home again (this happened with surprising frequency). Nobody knows how many died on the trail.

Smoke hung over the diggings like an endless fog. The only way they could penetrate the permafrost was to burn into it, loosen a few shovelfuls of earth and light the fires again. Of the 100,000 who had set out, about 4,000 found some gold, and a few hundred found a great deal. Charlie Anderson, the Lucky Swede, left the Klondike with £900,000, invested it in San Francisco real estate and lost the lot in the earthquake there. Dick Lowe had £500,000 at one time; he literally threw most of it away and spent the rest on women and drink. And Siwash George, in accordance with tight-lipped ideas of what should happen to a dropout who discovered the demon gold, was reported to have died a pauper in New York. In fact he did nothing of the kind. He took a fortune out of Rabbit Creek, used it to good effect and died a rich man.

In spite of all that has been won by blood and toil in the past 6000 years there has never at any time been enough gold to go round. This gap between supply and demand spurred innumerable attempts to manufacture it, and the quest to convert base metal into gold was still going on as late as 1750. There have been hundreds of charlatans and crackpots who sold formulas for producing it from a multitude of unlikely materials including eggshells, excrement and human hair, presumably blonde. Dishonest laboratories have foisted off debased gold and thinly plated metal on credulous customers. The search of the alchemists, however, was of a different order. Alchemy was a serious though misguided cul-de-sac of science, and in-

Left: *the Hub Saloon in Dawson City, with typical stand-up bar and brass footrail. Public Archives of Canada.*

tellectuals of the stature of Aquinas and Newton at least paid lip-service to it.

It sprang from the Aristotelian theory of matter, which is that everything, human beings, plants, the earth, water, is composed of the same basic substance, differing only in form as a result of evolution. Gold, being the noblest material, was therefore the most highly evolved. Continuing this logical chain, the alchemists believed that if iron or copper or lead were left long enough in the ground they would eventually evolve into gold: it was simply a question of time. What was needed was some process which would speed up the change. Alas, there was more symbolism than science in most of the experiments. The alchemists tried to marry 'male' and 'female' substances – sulphur the male and mercury the female – in the nuptial chamber of the crucible. From this union, they hoped, the long-sought philosopher's stone would emerge, the supreme catalyst that would change the lazy metals into gold.

Leonardo da Vinci rebuked the alchemists for these fanciful endeavours in the following terms:

By much study and experiment they are seeking to create not the meanest of Nature's products, but the most excellent, namely gold, true son of the sun, inasmuch as of all created things it has most resemblance to the sun. No created thing is more enduring than this gold. It is immune from destruction by fire, which has power over all other created things, reducing them to ashes, glass, or smoke. And if gross avarice must drive you into such error, why do you not go to the mines where Nature produces such gold, and there become her disciple? She will in faith cure you of your folly, showing you that nothing you use in your furnace will be among any of the things which she uses in order to produce this gold. Here there is no quicksilver, no sulphur of any kind, no fire nor other heat than that of Nature giving life to our world; and she will show you the veins of the gold spreading through the blue lapis lazuli, whose colour is unaffected by the power of the fire.

And examine well this ramification of the gold and you will see that the extremities are continuously expanding in slow movement, transmuting into gold whatever they touch; and note that therein is a living organism which it is not in your power to produce.

New sources of gold are nowadays almost as elusive as the secret of the crucible. With the usual irony that has accompanied his dealings with this extraordinary metal, man now has the power, in the form of controlled nuclear energy, to crack open gold-bearing mountains in an instant – if only he could find them. But the hidden lodes mock him, shrouded inside the enigmatic rocks. Everything the goldsmiths have ever produced, from their most triumphant masterpieces to the simplest of wedding rings, has been fashioned from gold that was won the hard way.

2

Goldsmiths of the Ancient World

The different civilisations of the ancient world were not water-tight cultural compartments. Ideas flowed from one into another; Egyptian motifs have been found on goldware in Etruscan tombs. Trade was a major source of communication. The Phoenicians ranged across the oceans, carrying with them other people's cultures at the same time as they carried trade goods. Conquest, too, led to an interchange of cultures. After the Persian armies had swarmed into Egypt in the 6th century B.C., Egyptian goldsmiths found work in the great new Persian capital of Persepolis.

As well as the interchange between nation and nation, there was within the different civilisations an interchange between the different arts. The goldsmiths may have been the most technically and artistically advanced of the metal workers, but they were not above borrowing ideas from the smiths who worked in copper and bronze. Much Persian jewellery is rooted in the stylised animal bronzes of Anatolia. The thriving ceramic industry of Crete also provided the Minoan goldsmiths with new forms and new decorative themes.

One problem which faces anyone writing about the goldwares of the ancient world is that of provenance. Many of the treasures of the past were unearthed before archaeology became a science. The amateur archaeologists of the 18th century were not too concerned to date their finds, even if they had had the means of doing so. The art of the past was considered as an end in itself, to be exhibited proudly, rather than as fragments of information, throwing a little more light on a dead and buried civilisation.

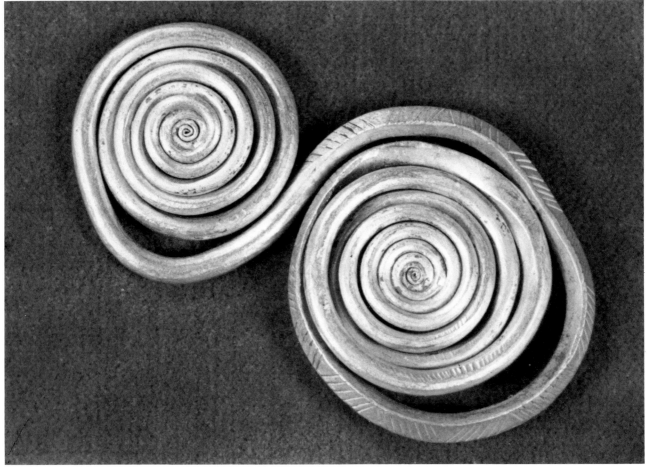

Those less respectable diggers, the tomb robbers and treasure hunters of the past, were at pains to conceal the sources of the finds they offered to private collectors and museums, and so many of the pieces of jewellery and goldsmithing of the ancient world that have escaped the melting pot can be given only presumptive sources and dates.

The problem is complicated by the ease with which goldwares can be successfully faked. Gold, because of its nobility, does not provide any simple clues to its age. The prohibitions imposed by some governments on foreign archaeologists have encouraged the faking of pieces in recent times. These spurious 'finds' have come onto the market as smuggled wares and found ready buyers. But the faking of ancient goldwares must, in fact, have been

Left, above: *gold bracelets from the Sacoşul Mare treasure, found in Romania. They are from the late Bronze Age and resemble in style Celtic ornaments found in Ireland.* Left, below: *Bronze Age gold ornament found in Romania.* Below: *repoussé gold dress ornaments called phalerae from Ostravul Mare, Romania. Middle Bronze Age. Bucharest Municipal Museum.*

carried out over the centuries. So long as there have been collectors there have been fakers to cater for them.

The greatest difficulty, however, facing anyone writing about the gold-wares of the ancient world is not provenance but paucity. Numberless goldwares must have been produced in Egypt over a period of 3,000 years, but all that is left are the contents of a dozen or so royal graves, the most important of which all belong to the Middle and the New Kingdoms. Only the innate conservatism of the Egyptian artists and the additional evidence provided by paintings and sculptures makes it possible to assess Egyptian goldsmithing on the basis of such slender evidence. And this is a recurring problem. So little is left to us from Ur, so little from Minoan Crete, so little even from Classical and Hellenistic Greece.

The Gold of the Egyptians

Only a few examples of Egyptian goldsmiths' work survive which were made before 3000 B.C. The earliest extant jewellery, discovered at the beginning of the present century by that great Egyptologist, Flinders Petrie, was in the grave of King Djer's wife at Abydos. She would have been buried about 3200 B.C. On her linen-wrapped arm four bracelets were still in position. They consisted of gold beads of various forms interspersed with beads of turquoise and lapis lazuli. In the centre of one bracelet is a gold rosette, the petals bent inwards like those of a half-open daisy. Another bracelet consists of oblong repoussé beads which look like façades of buildings, and on top of each is a bird, probably the Horus Falcon, which was one of the more important of the vast hierarchy of ancient Egyptian deities. These and other early finds, scanty though they are, suggest that goldsmithing had a long history in Egypt before 3200 B.C. The Egyptians had to start from scratch, and on the evidence of other civilisations their first attempts to work gold would have been to hammer nuggets to form crude, solid beads. When they eventually realised the need for annealing, and devised the technique, they would have been able to produce flat sheet work like that of the early British smiths and the Chavin Indians. Only later still would they have been able to produce enclosed forms like the symmetrical gold beads from Abydos and a few other protodynastic graves. This development could have taken many hundreds, even thousands, of years.

In *The Art and Architecture of Ancient Egypt*, W. Stevenson Smith writes: 'The Egyptian was interested in the outward look of living and inanimate things . . . He has a matter-of-fact rather than an imaginative attitude to the world about him, and when he deals with supernatural things manages with a kind of cheerful assurance to give them a similar, everyday look.' The Egyptian artist was also, as we shall see, unadventurous. He went on reproducing the same motifs, for the most part religious imagery and floral patterns, in much the same way. He refined rather than developed, and at no time since has art remained so static for so long. Surviving goldwares from the Middle Kingdom are almost exactly the same as those from the late Dynastic Period, over 1,000 years later, and most of the motifs were already fully developed as early as the Old Kingdom.

The most important finds from the Old Kingdom were made at Giza by an American group under G. A. Reisner in 1925. He discovered an undisturbed tomb, or cache, containing furniture belonging to Queen Hetep-heres, wife of King Sneferu and the mother of King Cheops. She had been buried about 2600 B.C., and the furniture indicates how lavishly gold was used in the royal households of the time. Components of a bed canopy (now re-erected in the Cairo Museum) are thickly sheathed in the metal, and the inner faces of the canopy portals are beautifully chased with hieroglyphs announcing Sneferu's titles and descent from the gods. The queen's name and titles are inlaid in gold in the ebony supports to a carrying chair, the pole ends of which are heavy gold palm terminals, derived from Egyptian architecture. A gold-sheathed box was also found, containing 20 silver bracelets graded in size. Though Egypt was rich in gold, there was no silver to speak of, and at some periods silverwares were the more highly prized.

A 4th Dynasty tomb of an unknown princess has been discovered at Giza. In this was found a diadem, a copper band to which a gold rondel of chased lotus buds is riveted. On either side of the rondel are double papyrus blooms with two ibises above. There was also a gold necklace of 50 repoussé beads in the form of beetles pendant from a wire. In these two 4th Dynasty finds, the dominant decorative elements which will reappear time and again in Egyptian jewellery are present – the hieroglyphs with their god symbols and boasts of power, and the stylised floral and animal forms. One other common motif is the abstract pattern, usually consisting of diamonds and zig-zags, and this is seen on a belt found at Saqqara in 1944.

Tomb paintings and sculptures provide further evidence of Egyptian fashions in jewellery. Men and women of the Old Kingdom royal households wore broad collars of many rows of beads, almost certainly of cornelian, turquoise and lapis, with oblong or rhomboid gold spacers. Women wore chokers, bracelets and anklets made in the same way, and both men and women wore diadems. The royal diadem, with a Uraeus serpent raising its head to strike, appears first in the art of this period.

Jewellery has been found in undisturbed tombs of the 11th and 12th dynasties. Though basically unchanged in style, it is more sophisticated and technically accomplished than the Old Kingdom examples. J. de Morgan found a pectoral of Senwosret III In 1894 at Dahshur. The pectoral was a boast of his prowess, and a talisman protected him from his enemies. It shows him, symbolised by two beasts with lion bodies and hawk heads, trampling the Nubians and the Libyans underfoot. Nekhbet the vulture goddess, the protectress of upper Egypt, holds a hieroglyph above the beasts, symbolising universal rule. The piece is made of a thick gold sheet, pierced out round the forms. Cornelian, turquoise and lapis are precisely cut in a variety of shapes to fit the cloisons. Egyptian jewellery, like the painting, is almost always two-dimensional. Only rarely are the forms

Above: *pectoral of Senwosret III, 12th dynasty. The beasts symbolise the king defeating the Libyans and the Nubians. It is set cloisonné, with cornelian, lapis lazuli and turquoise. Cairo Museum.*

Right: *Etruscan bracelet with extremely fine abstract granular decoration, and granules used to construct repoussé human figures. Vatican.*

given any volume, and when some modelling is attempted it is only in very low relief.

The next innovation in personal adornment was the introduction of ear-rings, and it took a period of chaos and an invasion to usher it in. The ear-rings probably arrived with the Hyksos, foreigners from the East who occupied Egypt during the troubles which followed the death of Amenemhet in 1797 B.C. During this time, as in all periods of upheaval, goldsmithing seems generally to have languished, however.

The New Kingdom, beginning with the 18th Dynasty, saw ordered life restored under strong Egyptian kings. This led to an artistic renaissance but by no means an artistic revolution. After a gap of 200 years the jewellers simply picked up the techniques and motifs of the past and employed them all over again. Indeed, it is hard to date Egyptian jewellery stylistically as pre-Hyksos and post-Hyksos. It is as though there had never been an invasion.

The most important of all Egyptological finds was Howard Carter's discovery of a virtually intact royal tomb of the New Kingdom in 1922. Under the patronage of Lord Caernarvon, he had been digging for five years in the Valley of the Tombs of the Kings, though his fellow archaeologists generally believed that the area had no more secrets to reveal. Rubble had previously been thrown down the hillside when the great tomb of Rameses VI had been excavated. And Carter had the thoroughness to investigate this débris. Beneath it he found a stairway of 16 steps, and at the bottom of them a doorway with the seal of the necropolis on it. He made a small hole, and by the light of a candle he got his first view of the treasures of Tutankhamun, an unimportant young monarch of the 18th Dynasty who had reigned for only a few years.

'As my eyes grew accustomed to the light', Carter wrote later, 'details of the room emerged slowly from the mist. Strange animals, statues and gold – everywhere the glint of gold.' When the doorway of the chamber was opened a few days afterwards, one of his colleagues described the place as 'an enchanted property room from an opera house of some great composer's dreams'. It proved to be only an ante-room. It contained three great wooden couches covered in gold sheet, a gold-clad throne enriched with gemstones, great chests and a jumble of smaller objects including golden bows and staves. The tomb had been disturbed by robbers at some time, but before they could ransack it they had presumably been surprised and the doorway resealed.

On either side of another door stood two lifesize wooden figures, partly

---

Left: *Queen Pu-abi's gold head-dress and ear-rings, found in her grave at Ur by Sir Leonard Woolley. British Museum.*

The death mask of Tutankhamun, sculpted from gold sheet and cloisonné set with lapis lazuli, cornelian and turquoise. Cairo Museum.

clothed in gold leaf, the guardians of the burial chamber beyond. Before opening this inner door Carter set about recording, removing and preserving the contents of the ante-room. When he at last entered the heart of the tomb

Left: *ear-ring from the Tutankhamun treasure, showing Minoan or Mycenean influence in the granular decoration.* Centre: *falcon pectoral from the tomb of Tutankhamun.* Right: *another ear-ring from the same source, the clasp decorated with the Uraeus, symbol of kingship. Cairo Museum.*

---

he found the biggest single collection of Egyptian gold work to survive: gold figures, gold-sheathed chariots, four gold-covered shrines, a vast hoard of jewellery and the sarcophagus itself.

Before he could open the sarcophagus, a bureaucratic dispute with the Egyptian government led to their sealing up the tomb, and to a law case which Carter lost. It was not until 1924 that he was able to return, when he found that the sarcophagus was in fact three coffins fitting one inside another. The inside one was of high carat gold, so heavy that four men could hardly lift it. Its lid represented the king in all his regalia, enfolded by the wings of protecting goddesses. The head of the mummy contained within it was covered by a gold death-mask which ranks among the great portrait busts of history. The body was covered in jewels, of which there were many more in the surrounding caskets.

Here for the first time the world could see why there was such an insatiable demand for gold in Ancient Egypt, why thousands of captives were kept slaving in the mines, why in spite of her own rich resources she searched so avidly for it abroad. If the interment of this minor king absorbed so much gold, how much must have been buried with such great rulers as Amenhotep III or Rameses II.

This mask and coffin demonstrate the complete mastery of their craft achieved by Egypt's court goldsmiths. By comparison the other treasures of Tutankhamun look like golden bric-a-brac, except of course for the exquisite jewellery. Among the jewellery there are two particularly beautiful pectorals. In one a cornelian-set sun symbol is enclosed by the vigorously upswept wings of a falcon; in the other by the wings of a scarab.

Ear-rings in this treasure provide interesting clues to possible foreign influence and technical development. One pair has fastenings in leech or boat form, popular in the Aegean. The fastenings and the beads are decorated with granulation, common on Mycenaean and Minoan jewellery. The motif of the pendant rings is a continuous spiral, again found in Greek areas. The granular decoration is of yellow gold, while other parts of the ear-rings are in red gold. Two repoussé pierced ornaments from the same find are also in red gold. Since the goldsmiths of the New Kingdom were capable of refining gold to a high purity, they may have deliberately alloyed their gold with copper to produce this coloured gold.

Among a number of undisturbed tombs discovered at Tanis in 1940 was that of King Psibkhenne I, who reigned 500 years after Tutankhamun. The jewellers of his reign were still employing the same old motifs and techniques. Of all the ornaments which Montet, the French Egyptologist, came across there, only three were outside the grand tradition. These were little gold pendants of the horned goddess Isis and of a lion and a bull with human bodies. All have the sun symbol above their heads and the uraeus serpent, the rearing cobra, on their brows. The rarest piece from Tanis was not jewellery but a gold vase (only a few other examples of Egyptian gold vessels survive). It is jug-shaped with a long tubular neck flaring out into a trumpet top chased with papyruses. Another remarkable gold portrait mask was found here. It depicts the sensuous face of General Wenw-djebaw-n-djedet.

Later vessels are represented by the vase of Ampelta, believed to have been made between 593 and 568 B.C., and a golden dish handle recovered at Daphnae. The vase is raised gold, of the amphora type, with a gold sheet handle chased with hieroglyphs down its length. The dish fragment has two bold palmettes derived from architecture and first seen 2,000 years earlier.

Jewellery found in Egypt of the period after 300 B.C. is completely Hellenised and could have been made in any Greek province; that dated after A.D. 30 is typical Roman provincial work.

Egypt was an astonishing civilisation which resisted change from the very dawn of history to the threshold of the Christian era. Now at last she could no longer resist change. As gold reflects light, so it can mirror the spirit of the society in which it was worked. The last gold of Egypt, with its weary formalism, its debased motifs and its generally perfunctory work-manship, shows that three centuries before the end the artists had lost heart. When the Egyptians finally surrendered their rigid traditions they had already merged themselves with the destiny of their conquerors.

Sumeria, Israel and Babylon

In 1922, while Carter was taking his first steps into Tutankhamun's tomb, Sir Leonard Woolley was staring at a six-foot-high mound in Mesopotamia, now Iraq. He had found it, he wrote, 'in the middle of a vast plain over which the shimmering heatwaves dance and the mirage spreads its mockery'. Here after five years of excavation he uncovered 'a maze of walls and well laid pavements of burnt brick . . . a four-square tower whose brickwork might be that of yesterday'. Here on the plain had stood Ur, one of the city-states of Sumeria. The tower was twin to the Tower of Babel, at the top of which the gods and goddesses resided, to be approached up soaring flights of steps.

The baked-clay tablets which Woolley dug out were laboriously written records of the people of Sumeria, their laws and customs and daily life in 2500 B.C. It was not, however, in the city but in the cemetery outside its walls that his most startling discoveries were made. Here, first of all, he unearthed gold beads. Then he found the grave of a man on whose skull still rested a beautiful repoussé helmet. From his silver-covered baldric, or shoulder belt, hung two sheaths, both decorated with finest gold filigree in pleasing geometrical patterns. One contained a gold toilet set – an ear-scoop, a head scratcher and tweezers on a silver ring. In the other was a superb dagger. 'The hilt', Woolley wrote, 'it made of a single piece of lapis lazuli studded with large drops of gold set in shallow depressions . . . No description is adequate to the sumptuousness and beauty of this weapon.' There were other gold-mounted daggers, a golden bowl and hundreds of the gold and lapis lazuli beads found all over the cemetery area.

Other discoveries in the cemetery included cast gold chisels, cast-chased gold amulets in the form of birds and a bull, and an adze and a finely burnished spearhead in an electrum alloy of 30 per cent gold and 60 per cent silver.

'Then came a discovery more strange and awe-inspiring than any archaeological find of the past century, apart from the tomb of Tutankhamun.' Woolley saw five bodies, then another group, 'those of them women carefully arranged in two rows; they wore head-dresses of gold, lapis lazuli and elaborate bead necklaces'. Across the remains of a harp

Above: *gold bowl from Ur made from two halves soldered together, and with a handle of twisted wire.* Right, above: *electrotype of a gold helmet found by Leonard Woolley at Ur, showing the Sumerian mastery of raising and repoussé chasing.* Right, below: *cosmetic bowl found at Ur, containing traces of eye make-up. British Museum.*

'lay the bones of the gold-crowned harpist'. He dug deeper, finding more bodies and treasure. A gold tumbler, fluted and chased, with a fluted feeding bowl, a chalice and a plain oval bowl lay piled together. 'The perplexing thing was that with all this wealth of objects we had found no body so far distinguished from the rest to be that person to whom all were dedicated.'

More of these macabre pits of death and riches were found. The tomb of King A-bar-gi was littered with bodies. Woolley found the remains of six soldiers, then of two wagons with oxen and drivers. Nine women wore headdresses from which gold beech-leaves dangled, necklaces and large gold earrings of the spiral form which can be seen in the British Museum. 'The

whole space between them and the wagons was crowded with other dead men and women, while the passage which led along the side of the stone chambers was lined with soldiers carrying daggers and with women.' All these people, chosen to die so that A-bar-gi should have a retinue in his tomb, seemed to have accepted their fate, walking into the pit dressed as for a gala. It is thought they took some drug and then lay down while the earth was thrown in on top of them.

The most beautiful gold objects of all came from the tomb of a queen originally identified as Shub-ad but whose name is correctly rendered as Pu-abi. There is a boat-shaped plain gold bowl with a handle of two twisted wires threaded through tubes soldered to the body. A feeding cup is also boat-shaped, with a spreading foot and a long curving spout. The body is boldly fluted and chased with a band of tiny chevrons, and a course of bolder chevrons at the rim. A gold tumbler, obviously raised from a flat disc of gold, is decorated in the same way.

Pu-abi's grave also contained a little footed gold goblet. As it has a protruding rim, and since craftsmen seldom make unpractical vessels, it is probably not a drinking cup but a specially designed holder for cosmetics, a suggestion which is borne out by what appears to be the remnants of green eye make up found in it. The head-dress on the queen's skull was a more magnificent version of those worn by her women attendants. From a complex arrangement of linked chain, beech-leaf pendants fell on her forehead. They rested on a wig, which in turn was fixed to a large wig-frame. Leonard Cottrell described it as 'a veritable flower garden' with gold rosettes between the leaves, their petals inlaid with lapis and white paste. A tall structure of gold strips ending in rosettes with lapis centres would have swayed above the queen's head.

The gold sheet used for these head-dresses is paper-thin, and they were unquestionably made for the burials, like so many Greek wreaths of a later period. More substantial were the gold and lapis collar necklaces worn by the queen and her women, and their gold earrings. The sheer mass of Egyptian funeral trappings was not echoed in Ur, probably because the Sumerians had to depend on imported gold. These two earliest gold-working kingdoms seem to have developed their skills and their artistry quite independently.

The biblical period in the Middle East was chaotic. Lands were conquered and reconquered, cities sacked and rebuilt, and multitudes slaughtered as the Babylonians, the Assyrians and the Egyptians held sway in turn. At times the Hittites, the Canaanites and the Israelites dominated limited areas. In the midst of all this turbulence the goldsmiths laboured away, making tableware, shields and golden thrones for the kings and sacred vessels and ornamentation for the temples. The temple of Solomon, according to the Bible, was 'overlaid with gold, also the whole altar'.

It is recorded that Solomon received 120 talents of gold from the Queen of Sheba. And in one year he is said to have received 'six hundred, three score and six talents, besides that which the chapmen brought and the traffic of the merchants'. That would amount to something like 36,000 lb of gold – more than the annual production of Rhodesia today. Even allowing for some exaggeration, he was well able to provide the rich embellishment for the great cedarwood edifice built for him by Phoenician craftsmen.

The treasures of Babylon, including those looted from the Temple of Jerusalem and profaned by Belshazzar's wives and concubines, were to turn up again when they were brought back as spoils to Constantinople in the Byzantine period. But after that they vanished for ever. We can only speculate that they may have been made in the tradition of the vessels from Ur. Or, in view of the strong Egyptian influence on the Sumerian city-states, some of them may have been lotus cups. At any event, time has washed away the work of all these craftsmen, or it lies buried under the modern cities of the region.

The Treasure of Troy

A lifelong conviction that the classical legends were based on fact led Heinrich Schliemann to dig up two of the most important gold hoards from the ancient world. A romantic German archaeologist, he was fascinated in boyhood by the Homeric tales. As he grew older he became increasingly convinced that the *Iliad* was not mere heroic fiction, but a history of great events. Schliemann was nevertheless a practical and successful businessman. He opened a bank in California during the big rush, bought gold dust, and added substantially to his fortune. In 1871, while still in his forties, he was rich enough to retire and devote his life to proving his theories about the past.

Schliemann's first objective was to locate the lost city of Troy, destroyed in the war which the legends attribute to the abduction of the beautiful Helen. He concluded that its site was at Hissarlik, a few miles from the mouth of the Dardanelles, and he employed 80 workmen to dig a wide trench into a hill there. His instinct proved correct, for before long they excavated the remains of 'the topless towers of Ilium'. In June 1873, by which time they had removed 230,000 cubic metres of soil, Schliemann noticed below one of these towers what looked like the gleam of gold. Prudently dismissing his workmen, he and his pretty Greek wife Sophia began to dig in the hard-packed earth. He feared that the wall above might collapse on them at any moment, 'but the sight of so many objects, every one of which is of inestimable value to archaeology, made me reckless'.

The objects included 8,700 gold rings, 60 gold ear-rings, a gold goblet weighing 601 grammes, and two gold diadems, one of which consisted of 16,353 individual pieces of gold. An engraving of the period shows Sophia wearing this diadem. It is of fine gold chain, from which 74 heart-shaped gold pendants hang in a fringe on her forehead. Sixteen longer pendants fall to her shoulders. She wears two other pieces composed of chain and the heart-shaped plates, and earrings in the same style. Also among the jewellery was a technically sophisticated bracelet, a wide strip of gold with overall filigree in continuous spirals.

Schliemann naturally assumed that this hoard had belonged to King Priam, who had perished with his city in the Trojan wars. Although it was afterwards proved to belong to a far earlier time, it is still known as 'Priam's treasure'. The skill and distinctive style of these early Anatolian gold workers was underlined in later finds by Turkish archaeologists at the royal tombs of Alaca Hüyük and at Dorak. Jugs, a cup and a wine goblet show how far they had progressed in raising complex forms from flat gold and in repoussé chasing. Compared with the exotic designs of Ur, the jewellery from these graves has a pleasing lightness and, as we might expect from the land of Helen, a charming femininity.

However, the restive Schliemann was not content with uncovering Troy. Soon he was to unearth a treasure which threw light on another lost civilisation.

Minoan and Mycenaean Gold

In 1876 Schliemann was still following the footsteps of Homer, and exploring a remote valley in the Peloponnese. Here had flourished Mycenae, the residence and burial place of Agamemnon, the capital of an important culture which reached its peak on the Greek mainland about 1600 B.C.

Schliemann's excavations in the ruins led him to a series of graves in the form of shafts. In one of them he discovered the bodies of three men with their gold weapons beside them, gold breastplates on their chests and golden death-masks covering their faces. 'Of the third body . . . the round face with all its flesh had been wonderfully preserved', he said. Fitting the facts to his dreams, he announced that he had 'gazed on the face of Agamemnon'. The mask that covered this face, with the rest of what he discovered, is now in the Athens National Museum. It shows a haunting face, strong, proud and regal, fringed with a luxuriant beard and curling moustache below an aquiline nose. Whoever this man was, he certainly had the bearing of a warlike king.

Left: *jug from the Oxus treasure. A similarly corrugated jug, but of native workmanship, was found on a site in Cornwall. British Museum.* Right: *fragment of a sword cast in the Mycenaean style found at Piersinari in Romania. Library of the Academy of the Socialist Republic of Romania, Bucharest.*

The goldwares from these graves are mostly plain shallow bowls, fluted beakers, and footed cups made from silver and gold. Only one or two of the grander cups show much decorative imagination. One has a repoussé frieze depicting a hunting scene running round it below the rim. Another has a circle of repoussé rosettes round the body. A footed gold cup found in one of the graves has little cast bird motifs on the terminals of its two handles, and pierced straps joining handles and base. This is the vessel to which Schliemann, starry-eyed as ever, gave the name of 'Nestor's cup'. (Nestor was the old king of Pylos who got home safely after the fall of Troy.) But it is a most improbable design. Neither the straps nor the birds seem to belong to it. Had its discovery by Schliemann not authenticated it beyond doubt, one would suspect it was the work of an inept faker.

Also among the graves he found a series of little spouted jugs and globular pots with lids which probably held the cosmetics, ointments and perfumes of the royal ladies. One of the objects he dug out depicted a bull's head, and this bull motif was to appear again and again on Mycenaean finds, incised into the tables of rings and on the sides of golden cups. The bull symbol is one of the key clues in tracing Mycenae's link with its counterpart, the Minoan civilisation.

The Minoans lived on Crete, in cities built closely around the palaces of Knossos and Phaestos. They developed the art of writing by substituting a linear script for the earlier hieroglyphs. An agricultural people, they had religious festivals in which bulls played a central part, including confrontations with young men who leaped over them. A mural showing this practice, so reminiscent of the legend of Theseus and the Minotaur, is one of the fascinations of the palace at Knossos. The so-called Vaphio cups, found in Laconia on the mainland of Greece, are flat-bottomed beakers with plain linings bent over to form the rims, on the outer casings of which the chase and capture of the wild bulls used for these festivals is shown in bold repoussé.

But besides a common interest in bulls, there are many other indications

Detail from a gold repoussé cup cup found at Vaphio in Greece, illustrating a bull hunt. National Museum, Athens.

that Mycenae and Minoa shared one culture, independent nations though they were. A ceramic cup from Phaestos (now in the museum at Heraklion) is of exactly the same form as the footed, loop-handled cups of gold and silver found at Mycenae. Marine motifs such as the dolphin and octopus are common to both places, and so is whorl decoration. This has been found both on gold box panels in the Mycenaean shaft graves and on Minoan jewellery.

Though the Minoan and Mycenaean goldsmiths were conservative in design, producing only a very limited number of patterns over a long period, they were highly competent and technically inventive. The Mycenaeans often enriched their silver vessels with gold plating or gold inlays. They applied gold foil to handles and rims. The gold was inlaid by cutting cloisons in the silver, applying a black substance – possibly powdered niello – and then placing the gold on top. The application of heat turned the niello into a bonding agent. A good example of this technique is the famous bronze dagger inlaid with a golden hunting scene.

The jewellers of these nations were much less inhibited than their gold-smith brothers, and from the Crete and Greece of the second millennium B.C. we have inherited jewellery in greater variety than from any of the other early civilisations. Hair ornaments from about 2500 B.C., found at Mochlos and now in the Metropolitan Museum in New York, are identical in style to the flower and leaf designs of the queen's head-dress from Ur. Diadems from Crete resemble one which Woolley picked up in the Sumerian city. As the first settlers in Crete came from Anatolia, which had close links with Sumeria, this is understandable. But after 500 years of growth, Minoan Crete made a great leap forward creatively. No longer relying on ideas from the mainland, she now began herself to influence her neighbours in the Middle East.

The most interesting pieces of Middle Minoan jewellery are the pendants, a number of which are in the Aegina treasure in the British Museum. One shows a human figure holding two ducks by the neck. Another shows two human heads, strongly modelled in repoussé, with hair swept back and curling behind the ears. Other pendants consist of broken hollow circles ending in two snouts, rather like miniature torcs. Within each circle two dogs sit on two monkeys, and seven delightful little cast hawks hang by their tails from tiny chains, alternating with seven discs. Another pendant, in the Heraklion Museum, has two hornets facing each other, their legs holding a ball decorated with granular work. These craftsmen also made simple finger rings, spiral ear-rings, hair and dress pins, and repoussé plaques pierced at the edges for sewing on the garments of the court ladies.

Jewellery of the late Minoan period is inseparable in style from that of mainland Greece. It includes mass-produced relief beads, mechanically turned out by hammering metal into a die or between a pair of punch tools.

Middle Minoan pendant from the Aegina treasure, made in about the 17th century B.C. *British Museum.*

Then, suddenly, about 1450 B.C., the Minoan civilisation was mysteriously wiped out. Whether Knossos and Phaestos were laid waste by the Mycenaeans, engulfed in an earthquake or tidal wave or, as some experts suspect, riven by the eruption of a submarine volcano, a great culture was extinguished. And soon afterwards Mycenae too was overwhelmed by invaders who came from the north as barbarians, but who were eventually to found the parent civilisation of our Western world – that of Greece. Before this happened, however, several other cultures were to rise and fall.

Phoenicians and Etruscans

The Phoenicians were probably an Arab tribe. They were one of the Canaanite peoples of biblical times who were allies of the Israelites over a long period.

They settled on the eastern coastline of the Mediterranean and built their cities, Tyre and Sidon chief among them, on promontories and offshore islands. Hemmed in as they were, they began to see their future as lying beyond the seas, influenced perhaps by settlers from Mycenae. The Phoenicians were the supreme businessmen and commercial travellers of the ancient world, and their trading posts swelled into cities in Cyprus and Malta, at Carthage and at Gades, the site of modern Cadiz.

Though, as has been said, the Phoenicians' contribution to goldsmithing was meagre, they were important as a bridge between the great gold cultures of Egypt and Mesopotamia and the later gold cultures of the West. Whatever they did in the arts was mongrel and derivative. All the way through to the 5th century B.C. they went on borrowing. On the belt from the Alisida treasure, found near Caceres in Spain, a man wrestling a lion is shown in repoussé, fringed with granulation. They took that motif from the Assyrians. Little pendants from Carthage feature the heads of Amon-Re the goat and Sekhmet the lion-headed. Both are Egyptian deities. Only occasionally, as on the embossed plaques of the Tharros bracelet in the British Museum, do we find Levantine motifs which could be native to the Phoenicians – but even these have the Horus eye from Egypt on their ends.

Though lacking in invention, the Phoenician goldsmiths were competent craftsmen. They are known to have set up workshops in Greek cities and taught local apprentices between 800 and 600 B.C. And much Greek jewellery of that period, owing to their relaying of ideas, is completely oriental in style.

Where there were trading fleets, it was fated that sooner or later they would attract pirates. The Etruscans managed to combine piracy with a great love of music, and honest hard work with sensual and intellectual appetites. In their puzzling but somehow balanced civilisation, according to Aristotle, they 'fought, kneaded dough and beat their slaves to the sound of a flute'. There are a number of theories about where they came from. One holds that they migrated from famine in Lydia; another that they were a native Italian people. But there is much evidence to suggest that they were in fact of Oriental origin, and their language, their burial habits and their taste in jewellery seem to support this.

They appeared about 900 B.C. in Umbria and spread along the shores of the Tyrrhenian Sea, between the Arno and the Tiber. They were governed by a rich and self-indulgent aristocracy of princes and by a gloomy religion. The tombs of these princes were at first furnished with bronze utensils and armour, then painted and supplied with imported, or pirated, luxuries.

Very few gold vessels have been found in the tombs, but they were rich with gold jewellery, of which almost every conceivable type was made in Etruria. Foreign craftsmen were installed to keep up the flow of personal ornaments, and there seems to have been no restriction on their imagination or ingenuity. The Etruscans were wonderfully adept at filigree work and their repoussé decoration, particularly after 400 B.C., was equal to that of the Hellenistic Greeks. But it was in granular decoration that they particularly excelled, bringing it to a quality never seen before or since. They lavished

Disc from a heavily granulated Etruscan ear-ring, 6th century B.C. *Schmuckmuseum, Pforzheim.*

Right, above: *Roman gold bars stamped at the mint at Sirmium with the Proconsular mark and the mark of the mintmaster. 4th century* A.D. *British Museum.* Below: *Etruscan bowl covered with granular work which gives it a silken patina. Victoria and Albert Museum, London.*

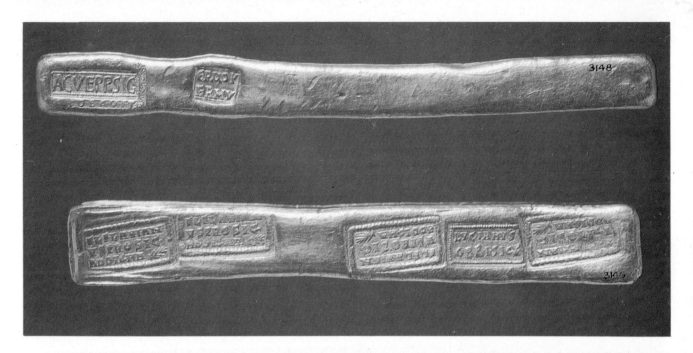

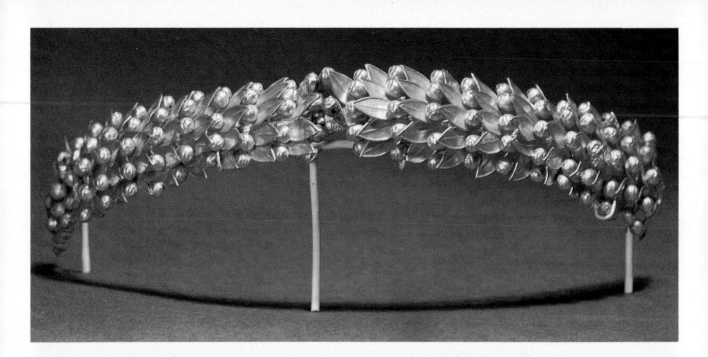

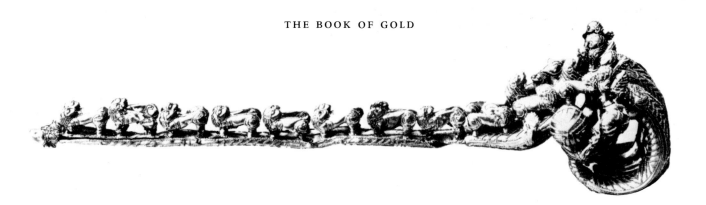

Etruscan fibula found at Vulci. It dates from the 7th century B.C. *and is decorated with a parade of animals covered with granulation. British Museum.*

---

all their skill on the fibula, which began as a simple safety-pin for fastening a cloak. Two main types have been differentiated, the serpentine, and the leech or boat type.

A very ornate example of the serpentine type is in the British Museum collection. Dating from the 7th century B.C., it is a long bar ending in a twisted bow and decorated with chevrons of fine granular work. Parading up it on to the bar are lions, horses and sphinxes in the round, encrusted with more granules. There is another in the Vatican Museum which must be the most magnificent safety-pin ever produced. One might easily fail to recognise it as a pin at all, so overlaid is it with ornament. The bow again has a parade of animals in the round. A large plate covers the foot, embossed with five repoussé lions and surrounded on the outside by two bands of stylised floral decoration. The most unusual feature of this fibula is the centre section, two transverse tubular elements decorated all over with chevrons and ending in Hellenistic-style pendants. One wonders what the cloak must have been like that was fastened with such splendour. The granules are so fine on some of these Etruscan fibulae that as many as 180 are laid to the linear inch.

Judging by paintings and sculptures, every Etruscan woman wore ear-rings, of which the characteristic form is the baule or bag. Their necklaces are fringed with a mass of repoussé pendants in acorn or vase designs, or with the bearded head of Silenus. An Etruscan pendant (in the Louvre) of Achelous, the horned river god, recalls the 'Agamemnon' mask from Mycenae. Bracelets were cut from sheet gold and decorated with repoussé,

---

Left, above: *Etruscan myrtle wreath, about 5th century* B.C. *British Museum.* Below: *fluted feeding cup from Ur, decorated with chased linear decoration. British Museum.*

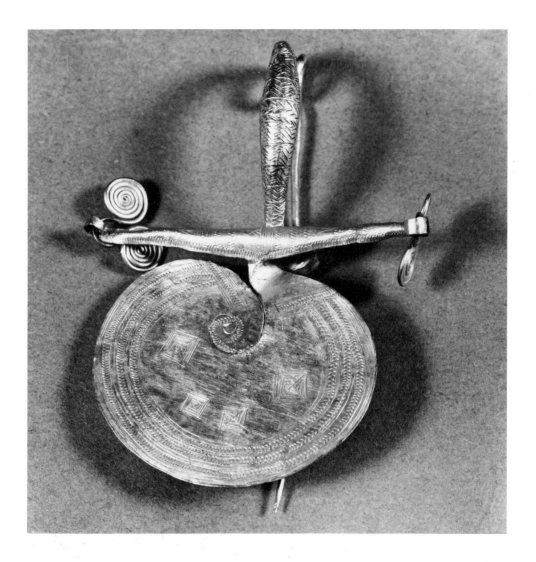

Above: *7th-century Etruscan fibula of the leech or boat type.* Right: *Etruscan necklace, 5th century* B.C. *British Museum.*

granular work or bands of open-work filigree. Hairpins had ball tops covered with a mass of granules. Rings included swivel types set with engraved scarabs.

The tableware found in the tombs has nothing to connect it with the unfettered originality of the jewellers. Silver gilt bowls show Egyptian battles and processions of Greek horses on the same vessel – suggesting that their makers were those artistic magpies, the Phoenicians. Other vessels

have Assyrian motifs or Greek key patterns over Egyptian-style lotus flower bases. These objects may have been booty from Carthaginian galleys, or trade goods exchanged for iron, zinc, tin and copper from the Etruscan hills. In either case, the poverty of these imported ideas only emphasises the brilliance of the native artists.

Of all the ancient world's jewellery, that of Etruria is the most imaginative, and the technical skill of its makers was unparalleled. When the Romans finally swept away Etruscan culture the art of the goldsmith declined in Italy. It was not to reach such heights again until the Renaissance.

The Bounty of Persia

The Persian empire, assembled by conquest in the middle of the first millennium B.C., was a loose and liberal arrangement compared with the systematic, disciplined unity the Romans later imposed on their empire. It was deliberate Persian policy to let the 29 vassal states pursue their own political, religious and cultural lives, provided they continued to bend the knee and pay tribute. As a result what is called Persian art is a blend of many regional streams. Coming together at the centre of the empire, in such projects as the building and furnishing of great palaces like Persepolis, these streams did evolve into a distinctive Persian style, but even there it remained a derivative one.

Archaeological discoveries suggest that the majority of the Persian court goldsmiths were either Egyptian or Median. Sometimes the influence of both these cultures can be seen on a single piece. A type of vessel very common among surviving Persian work is the rhyton, combining a bowl with an animal figure. Distinctively northern in style, these rhyta were probably the speciality of the Medians. Only one surviving example looks like Egyptian work. Found at Ecbatana, this is a fine standing rhyton with a base in the form of a winged lion crouching. The wings, chased on gold sheet, have the same rhythmic pattern as the cloisonné wings on Tutankhamun's breastplate.

All the other known rhyta are in the naturalistic style of the craftsmen of the north. The favourite subject of these craftsmen were goats, sheep and various kinds of deer. The muzzles delicately sniff the air and the eyes have the gentle limpid character of these shy creatures. The modelling, repoussé chased on raised beaker shapes, is very fine. These are superb essays in goldsmithing, and artistically vigorous as later work seldom is.

Persian jewellery varies so much in design and quality that it is difficult to define a Persian style at all. One form closely associated with Persia, however, is the penannular, or broken circle, bracelet with animal head finials, the forerunner of the Celtic torcs of western Europe.

The largest find of Persian gold work is the Oxus treasure, believed to have been a temple hoard of the 5th or 4th century B.C. It was discovered near the river Oxus, which rises south of Samarkand. The local villagers sold the treasure to Moslem merchants, but the 19th-century traveller Captain

Right, above: bracelet with gazelle terminals, about 5th century B.C. Below: amulet with cloisonné decoration from the Oxus treasure. Most of the cloisons were empty when it was found. British Museum.

F. C. Burton eventually recovered it piece by piece. It is now in the British Museum. There are a number of torc-form bracelets and necklaces with cast animal head terminals, formed from a single square-sectioned rod of gold, or from gold wire wrapped around a core. The heads resemble those on the rhyta but were cast and chased up. Several little horses had been cast, but in four others drawing a chariot the legs have been bent up from sheet gold and soldered on. Vignettes of Persian life of the period are scribed on many thin oblong plaques. The Oxus hollowares include a jug with horizontal faceting on the body, and a cast handle with a lion's head. Rearing lions and lotus buds appear in repoussé on a shallow bowl which is a predecessor of the Greek phiale mesomphalos.

Most of these pieces are of poor quality and artistry, and a similar provincialism marks the Ziwiyeh treasure now in the Teheran Archaeological Museum. Scythian influence shows in this collection, in repoussé griffon and lion mounts for furniture and harness, and in a thin gold sheet pectoral of leech form, with a procession of animals in low relief. One of several rondels found at Ziwiyeh depicts the Assyrian hero-god, Gilgamesh, holding two lions upside down by their feet, like a hunter with a couple of rabbits. A penannular bracelet is more complex than other examples. It is a fluted D-shaped tube which develops into two ornamental triangles with two chased lozenges below. One of its lion's head terminals can be removed by drawing out a gold pin, to allow the bracelet to be fitted and fastened.

These finds from the edge of the empire may not be representative. The lost work of metropolitan Persia may have been quite different in style and quality. But this provincial work is proof, none the less, despite the often inferior execution, that virtually every technique known today was available to the men who fashioned gold within this great empire 2,500 years ago.

Repoussé chased mount typical of the workmanship of the north of the Persian Empire, and probably dating from the 5th century B.C. *It sold for £1,900 ($4,560) in 1970.*

The Greeks and Their Neighbours

The early Greeks were never very rich in gold, and they had to make do with a silver coinage. The only supplies available to their goldsmiths in the early days would have been melted down from the plunder the Greeks had taken from the Mycenaeans. It was only after Alexander the Great overthrew the Persians in the 3rd century B.C., acquiring booty and bullion, that they could issue gold coins in any quantity, commission gold plate for their tables, and jewellery for their women. Throughout their history the Greeks kept up the tradition of decking-out the royal dead with gold – but these funeral trappings were paper thin. In Greece, reverence had to go hand in hand with economy.

About 800 B.C. the Phoenician craftsmen introduced the Greeks to motifs from Egypt and Babylonia, setting up workshops in mainland cities and the kingdoms of Rhodes and Crete, and inaugurated the so-called Egyptianising

Greek necklace plaques showing strong Egyptian influence, made in the 7th century B.C. *and found at Rhodes. British Museum.*

period of Greek art. Another source of the foreign influences perceptible in Greek goldsmithing may have been Delphi, where pilgrims from many parts came to make offerings and consult the Oracle. It was perhaps through these offerings that Greek goldsmiths became acquainted with such characteristically Persian forms as the rhyton, the phiale and the deep Achaemenid bowls, versions of which they were to produce over a period of many centuries.

The Persian phiale were bowls swelling at the base with a central boss called the omphalos. Early Greek equivalents seem to have been usually of silver, plain, with no more than a frieze of repoussé acorns round the boss. Later, more decorative ones were made, and some in gold have survived, including an example decorated with three courses of negroid heads. The rhyta, like the Persian originals, consist of an animal head base out of which the cup develops. But their repoussé decoration is typically Greek, showing scenes from mythology. The Judgment of Paris is depicted on one surviving Greek rhyton, and Herakles and Theseus appear on another. All these Greek wares based on Persian models were almost certainly ritual vessels, and their survival may result from the practice of hiding the treasure of the shrines in safe places during periods of strife. It was not only fear of capture by an enemy that suggested such precautions; as has been noted previously, Greek leaders in a gold-starved state were not above removing sacred objects to pay for their campaigns.

Neither of the great religious statues created by Pheidias in the 5th century B.C. has survived. His Athena at Athens was 35 ft high, and was said to have been of ivory covered with 2,000 lb of removable gold sheet. The Zeus at Olympia was also of ivory, clothed in gold robes. The god had golden sandals and sat on a golden throne. Pheidias must, one imagines, have had to melt down a great mass of gold plate and jewellery from the shrines to obtain the gold for his gigantic images.

Many early Greek gold wares have been found in south Russia, and more were unearthed a few years ago at Panagyurishte in southern Bulgaria. One would not expect gold-working to have flourished among nomadic barbarians; but the Scythians and Sarmatians, who were always threatening the northern boundaries of the settled civilisations, had a great fondness for gold.

The nomadic chiefs were important patrons of the Greek goldsmiths, some of whom worked in Scythian territories using alluvial gold from the Urals. They made gold decorations for the chiefs' tents, and plaques to be sewn on clothes and harness. There is a particularly fine piece in the Hermitage Museum in Leningrad, dating from the 5th century B.C. and found in the Crimea. It has a repoussé lion, stag and griffon on the body and a crouching dog under the neck. In the same museum is a plaque of the Sarmatian tribe showing three figures under a tree to which two horses are tethered. A

Golden helmet dating from the 5th century B.C., *discovered at Cotofenesti, Romania. Its repoussé decoration is believed to have magical significance. Bucharest National Museum. Below: plaque in the form of a crouching stag; Scythian, from the Ziwiyeh treasure. Hermitage, Leningrad.*

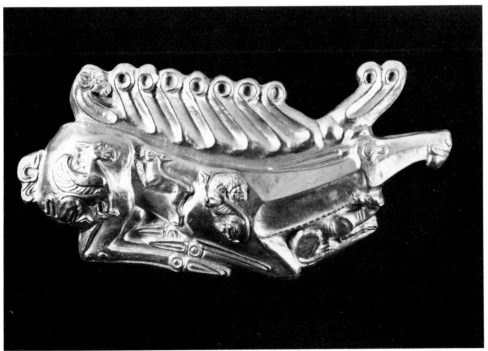

This page, above: *Sarmatian gold plaque from the 1st millennium* B.C. *Hermitage, Leningrad.* Below: *this western Greek fibula from the 4th century* B.C. *has an elaborate coiled pin. British Museum.* Right: *late Nomadic work from the Sarmatian Kholach treasure, 2nd century* A.D. *Hermitage, Leningrad.*

burial mound at Maikop contained the skeleton of a chief who had died before 2000 B.C. The wooden-walled chamber contained gold beads and vessels and a diadem with rosettes, as well as a splendid canopy frame of gold and silver rods slotting into each other. There were also 89 gold plaques of lions and bulls for displaying on the tent of this travelling king. The Bulgarian find included four gold rhyta with bases in the shape of a stag, a bull, a goat and a ram. As these tribes moved southward from the steppes, designs in the manner of the Greeks and the Persians appeared increasingly on their scabbards and bowcases.

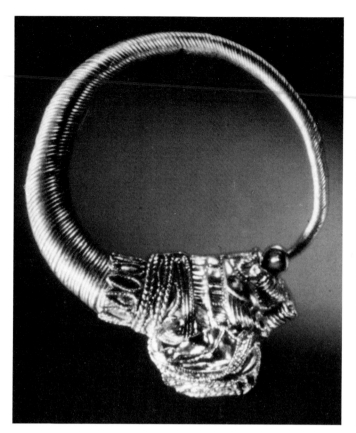 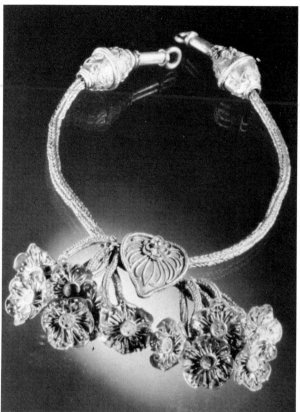

The so-called Hellenistic period began with Alexander the Great. By
300 B.C. the upheavals following his death had given way to order, and
when we speak of Hellenistic Greece we are no longer referring to a rocky
peninsula with a necklet of islands, but to a widespread empire. Greek
culture spread far beyond these boundaries. Carthage was now as Greek as
Syria or Egypt. This period saw the production of some of the most impressive
jewellery in history. It had its roots in the earlier classical period, but the
gold of Persia enabled the Greek workers to make lavish pieces in quantity,
in a sensuous, opulent style designed to appeal to a newly rich people.

Technically the Hellenistic smiths were outstanding. Their casting and
repoussé work was a miniaturisation of the great Greek sculptors' achievements in stone and bronze. They handled filigree decoration with the same
mastery that the Etruscans had brought to granular work. And they used
gemstones and enamel to give their pieces an even stronger mood of luxury.
Functional jewellery such as pins and fibulae seems to have gone out of
fashion, and the women demanded elaborate diadems, necklaces, rings and
ear-rings. Rings with large bezels set with cabochon stones, usually garnets,
were probably an innovation of the Hellenistic workshops. Ear-rings were
pendants in the form of amphorae, enamelled birds, roses and figures on

Far left: *ear-ring in the form of a stirrup with horned lions' heads on the clasps. Greek, 4th century* B.C. *Left: Greek necklace from Asia Minor, 4th century* B.C. *It has a plaited gold chain and quite realistic flowers hanging from a heart-shaped granulated plaque. Above: serpent bracelet with a garnet in a knot. Greek, about 300* B.C. *Schmuckmuseum, Pforzheim.*

chains. Necklaces had pendants in the shape of little vases, and a flat woven ribbon chain supplanted the link chain of classical times.

The lavishness of Hellenistic jewellery is illustrated by a golden diadem of the 2nd century B.C., found at Kerch in southern Russia and now to be seen in Munich. The centrepiece is a knot of Herakles, a motif first used in Minoan Crete, of skilfully polished garnets in a gold setting. These are held in place by small tongues of gold and four collars decorated with filigree. Above the knot is a cast Winged Victory supported on either side by writhing sea-serpents. Below the knot are three pendants consisting of garnet beads hanging from filigree medallions. The circlet of the diadem is of gold tube, richly decorated and hinged to the central motif.

In view of the quite substantial amount of jewellery that has survived, it is disappointing that so little of the Hellenistic goldsmiths' tableware and

Cup found at Tirana, with a continuous pattern of naturalistic birds consuming worms, snakes and other prey. Archaeological Museum, Istanbul.

religious work has been uncovered. Indeed, from this period only silver-gilt two-handled drinking cups, vases, jugs and bowls remain to indicate what may once have existed in gold.

The Disappointments of Rome

Rome at the beginning was even poorer than Greece. In 390 B.C. the entire gold reserves of the Republic amounted to less than a seventh of the offering King Croesus sent to the Delphic Oracle. The Romans had little silver, and their coinage at this time was of bronze. Under a law of the 3rd century B.C. no Roman woman might wear more than half an ounce of gold, and only a few privileged persons such as senators and knights were allowed to wear gold rings – and only on special occasions. It is not surprising that no distinctive Roman style of goldsmithing was evolved until the Greek empire had fallen and Spain was occupied. But even when Rome at last had ample gold at her disposal from East and West, other calls were always being made upon these reserves. The huge and restless Roman empire had endless military commitments, and the luxuries imported from the whole known world had to be paid for in gold.

Up to about 30 B.C. Roman jewellery, what there was of it, was either late Etruscan or Hellenistic in style. Surviving pieces are nearly all poor in quality and uninspired in design, marking the end of the great eastern tradition. Inspiration is flagging, the old high standards of workmanship have given way to shoddiness, and, like much Roman art, there is a heavy vulgarity about it. This indeed is true of Roman jewellery as a whole, though among later work there are a few pieces which are well made and of some artistic merit.

The Romans have to be credited with developing two important decorative techniques, though they did not invent them. The first of these was the pierced work called *opus interrasile*, later perpetuated in Byzantine jewellery. This decoration was produced by cutting away metal with a chisel, the laborious method used as late as the 18th century for the tops of casters. A bracelet of the 4th century A.D. in the British Museum features *opus interrasile* work as a surround to chased hunting and vinting scenes. The second technique was niello work, a form of champlevé enamelling but consisting of black linear patterns instead of coloured arabesques.

The Romans gave colour to their jewellery by setting it with emeralds from Egypt, agates from Sicily and Germany, garnets from eastern Europe. They had a wider range of gemstones than is seen in any earlier jewellery. And they made the stones the most important part of their most effective pieces, the settings being merely a means of displaying them to the best advantage. Typical is a lovely chain necklace in the Museo Nazionale in Naples set with uncut emerald crystals and mother-of-pearl cabochons. An early example in the British Museum has a butterfly pendant set with garnet, sapphire, emerald and quartz crystal.

Left: *Roman ring with* opus interrasile *decoration, 4th century* A.D. *Schmuckmuseum, Pforzheim. Below: Roman ear-rings showing styles popular from the 1st to the 3rd centuries* A.D. *Those to the right are from the eastern corners of the Roman Empire.*

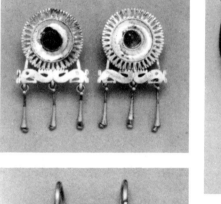

Right: *a rare Roman hollow-ware known as the Harewood gold vase, dating from the 1st century* A.D. *It was sold in London in 1965 for 11,000 guineas ($27,700).*

Perhaps because of the previously mentioned restrictions, rings eventually became a favourite form of jewellery in the Roman world. Even if we do not take Martial too seriously when he writes of a man who wore six rings on every finger day and night, he is obviously satirising a contemporary fashion (one which, incidentally, was to reappear among young people of the West in the late 1960s). Rings were also a symbol of betrothal among the Romans. Others, with imperial portraits, sometimes golden coins set in a bezel, may have been conferred by the emperors as rewards. Rings have been found with heads formed by a number of stones in separate settings. Solitaires were fairly common, and there are versions of the modern enternity ring with stones set all around the shank.

A popular type of Roman ear-ring was a gem-set medallion with gem-set pendants hanging from a bar below it, while the old serpentine bracelets first seen in the East were worn by Romans as late as the 1st century A.D.

Although a good many Roman silverwares have come down to us, one may search almost in vain for Roman gold cups, bowls and plates. Two rare

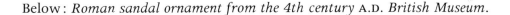

Below: *Roman sandal ornament from the 4th century* A.D. *British Museum.*

Left: *shoulder clasp decorated with cloisonné enamel from the Sutton Hoo ship burial. British Museum.*

surviving examples are probably not typical of what was produced as they seem too austere to have appealed to Roman taste, a taste which the makers of silverwares such as the Mildenhall treasure so obviously catered for. The Harewood Vase, so-called from its association with the Earls of Harewood, is an 11 in-high gold Roman vase from about 100 B.C. Completely plain and club-shaped, its form is obviously derived from pottery. A very similar vase, but somewhat smaller, is in the British Museum.

Rome provided posterity with no great burial hoards. Our information about Roman work has come piecemeal from corners of that vanished empire: a few trifling bits of jewellery from tombs in Lyons, Carlisle and Tarsus; a ring from the ruins of a Gloucestershire villa, perhaps overlooked by its owner when the Romans left Britain; a handful of pieces abandoned by the fleeing people of Pompeii. If these finds are typical, and there is no reason to think they are not, then we must conclude that Roman goldsmithing was a disappointing climax to a great tradition of the ancient world.

A Roman bracelet dating from the 2nd or 3rd century A.D. *The eagle was probably made in the eastern part of the Empire in the 3rd or 4th century* A.D.

From the Fall of Rome to the Renaissance

The Jewels of the Barbarians

Barbarian is a convenient label applied to works of art produced in Europe between the fall of Rome and A.D. 1000. It suggests that this art was crude, whereas in fact the Barbarian goldsmiths were men of imagination and skill, and masters of both filigree and cloisonné work.

The chaos of the times is reflected in their work, with Roman, Byzantine, Celtic and nomadic influences intermingling. Their output included objects as varied as the Lombardic 6th-century Cross of Agilulf in Monza cathedral, the 4th-century bird brooch from the Pietroasa treasure in Bucharest, and the 6th-century Nordic collars in the Statens Historiska Museum in Stockholm.

The Monza cross, enriched with important cabochon stones in box settings and its ball pendants, is entirely in the spirit of Byzantium. The three-dimensional Pietroasa brooch, set with stones (usually garnets), glass or rich red translucent enamel, is one of the earliest surviving examples of what in Britain is called the Anglo-Saxon style. The finest examples of

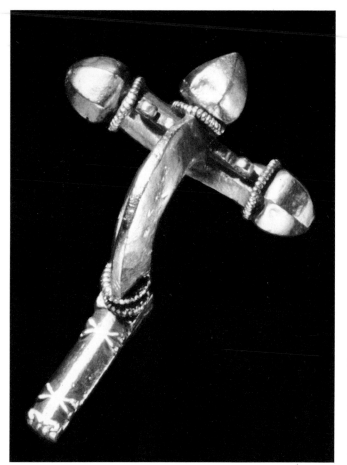

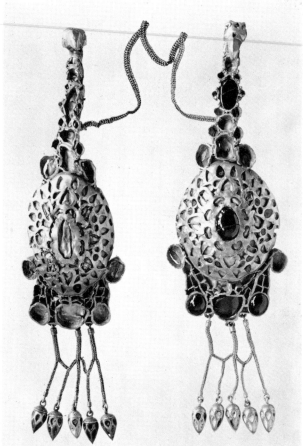

Opposite, above left: *Roman fibula from the 5th century* A.D. *Schmuckmuseum, Pforzheim.* Above right: *linked brooches in the form of birds of prey, cloisonné set with garnets. From the Pietroasa treasure, Romania, 4th century* A.D. Below: *this octagonal gold cup with panther handles is one of a pair from the Pietroasa treasure, originally set with gemstones, probably garnets.* This page, left: *detail of a gold brooch from the Pietroasa treasure. Bucharest National Museum of Antiquities.* Right: *chased gold buckle from the Sutton Hoo treasure. British Museum.*

---

this are the pair of 7th-century shoulder brooches found in Britain in the Sutton Hoo ship burial, in which central European, Viking and Celtic conventions can be discerned. One of the Nordic collars is the work of an extremely resourceful craftsman. He turned three stout gold tubes on a lathe to form a series of fluted bosses along their length. Next, he bent up the tubes and soldered them together. At the junctions he soldered on human masks and little beasts, reminiscent of nomadic work, and finally he decorated the whole piece with twisted wire filigree which is reminiscent of Hellenistic jewellery.

Indeed the Barbarian period was neither a cultural desert nor a clean break with the past. The mainstream of goldsmithing tradition continued to flow from East to West, and on the old themes and techniques some vigorous styles were built. Even in an age of almost ceaseless fighting, the jewellery made by barbarian artists for the warring Germanic chieftains and their queens often had considerable charm.

Frankish decorative disc set with gems and mother-of-pearl, about 4th century A.D. *Schmuckmuseum, Pforzheim.* Below: *Frankish gold fish ornament, 6th century* A.D. *Victoria and Albert Museum, London.*

The Golden Arts of Byzantium

The Byzantine empire lasted from the 6th to the 15th centuries, and at its zenith Constantinople was a glittering city. It was the eastern capital of the Roman world and the chief gold mart of the day. The furniture in Justinian's palace was covered with gold, and golden lamps and candelabra hung from the ceilings. Goldsmiths' workshops were busy everywhere within the walls, and one emperor, Constantine VII, even tried his hand at the craft.

The churches of Byzantium, with their round arches and rotund domes, were the most spectacular achievements of this culture, and the big mosaics on their walls were scattered with gold. Mosaic, wrote Eric Newton, is 'the perfect vehicle for visual symbolism on a large scale'. Much Byzantine gold-smithing has the same simple boldness and direct appeal of contrasting colour blocks, and the jewellers used a mosaic style for some of their designs, setting little pavements of stones cloisonné in a gold frame. A 7th-century ear-ring in Naples, for example, displays a woman's head in this mode.

The Roman *opus interrasile* work was most popular among patrons of Constantinople's artists. In 1970 two hexagonal pendants in this idiom,

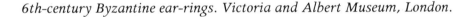

6th-century Byzantine ear-rings. Victoria and Albert Museum, London.

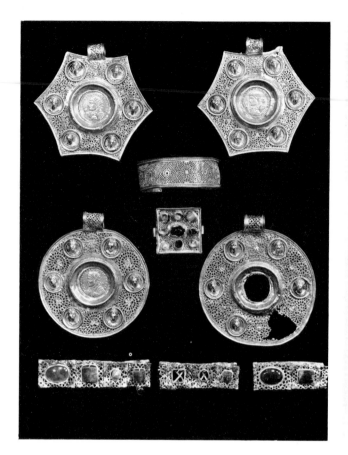

Above left: *four gold* opus interrasile *pendants containing fine Byzantine gold double solidi of Constantine the Great, and the fragments of a gem-set* opus interrasile *bracelet. The* opus interrasile *work is probably later in date than the 4th-century coins, The four pendants sold for a total of £45,000 ($109,200) in London in 1970. The bracelet sold for £5,250 ($12,600).* Above right: *a very fine Byzantine* opus interrasile *pendant on a disc necklace, dating from the 5th or 6th century* A.D. *It was sold in London in 1970 for £480 ($1,145).* Right: *Golden altar from Aachen Cathedral, with repoussé panels in a wooden frame. Made about 1000* A.D.

each 3.75 in across, were sold at Christies, together with a circular pendant. All three were mounted with specimens of the beautiful gold coinage of the empire, the double solidi of Constantine the Great. There was also a much finer example of gold work in the same sale, a necklace of linked discs with a pierced medallion.

Mosaics were the inspiration too for many of the gold Byzantine gospel covers, one of which is in the San Marco treasury in Venice. A comparison between this 11th-century masterpiece and the overloaded, incongruous

Renaissance covers testifies to the superiority of the Constantinople artists in producing designs which evoked the spirit of the holy texts contained within them. The San Marco cover has a central panel with the figure of an angel wearing a cope heavily set with stones. The head is ringed with a nimbus. The range of techniques shows this piece to be from a workshop that employed experts in every branch of the craft. Filigree, granulation, repoussé, chasing and cloisonné enamelling combine to give a variety of texture and colour. But despite this virtuosity, the design has the direct appeal and strength of great ecclesiastical art.

Church work in the Byzantine style was also carried out in Italy, where Adrian I commissioned a golden candelabrum for St Peter's in Rome in the 6th century. It held 1,465 candles. Coptic Egypt and eastern Europe, right across to southern Russia, were further strongholds of this tradition. In the end Constantinople was sacked and its treasures borne off in the name of religion by soldiers of the Fourth Crusade in 1204. This pillage was accompanied by inhuman butchery, the Crusaders who followed the dour creed of St Paul holding that the people of Byzantium, following the Greek rite, had overreached themselves in earthly splendour and must be subdued. What little was overlooked by the pious looters was carried off by the Turks who captured the city in 1453 when the empire finally fell to Islam.

But for centuries after this imperial crowns and church furniture continued to be made in the Byzantine style elsewhere, including Russia, until the later empires vanished in their turn.

Left: *gem-set gold cross with a cameo of a Caesar. 10th century. Treasury of Aachen Cathedral.*

British and Irish Gold

As early as 2000 B.C. the neolithic peoples who had established themselves in northern and southern England, in Scotland and in Ireland were producing gold wares with a distinctive style of their own. At first, simple shapes like lunulae, crescent-type neck ornaments, were cut from gold sheet and normally left undecorated. The famous cape, found at Mold in Flintshire, is a marked advance on these ornaments and is probably later in date. It is shaped up from a large sheet of gold into a covering for the arms, chest and back of the wearer. But the course upon course of repeated repoussé motifs,

---

Repoussé gold cape, probably from the 1st millennium B.C. *British Museum.*

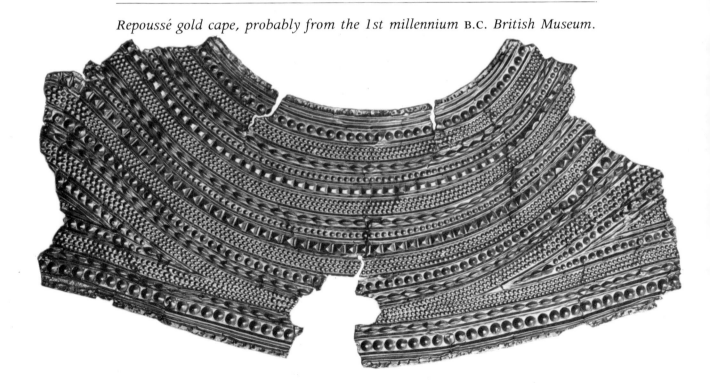

101

flutes, diamonds and squares, further enriched with bright dot work, is a new sophistication. At the sides, where the cape is shaped to the body, a dart motif such as a dressmaker might employ is an interesting refinement. It allows the goldsmith to retain the rhythmical order of the repoussé courses at front and back. This competent and imaginative work exhibits the self-assurance of a man with a long-established tradition behind him.

The Celts introduced new ideas to the islands after about 600 B.C. or perhaps even earlier. Among these early goldsmiths the Irish were outstandingly accomplished. They enjoyed more than local fame. Their work has been found in graves all over the United Kingdom, and it also obviously influenced English craftsmen. From about 1200 B.C. Eastern forms appeared, and jewellery became three-dimensional. Little penannular earrings of coiled wire, found in Ireland and Northumberland, are similar to those that were popular in the eastern Mediterranean.

The most important new form, however, was the torc, which reached Britain and Ireland from the East via the nomadic tribes of the Continent. These wrist and neck ornaments of twisted wire were made in large numbers, judging by the quantity recovered from graves. Most are simpler in style than the Eastern examples that inspired them, though others, like the Tara torc from the isle of Axholme in Lincolnshire, are more complex. In this necklet, a piece of square-sectioned gold rod has been twisted, rounded at the ends and bent back on itself to form a clasp. Three little rings of twisted gold wire were threaded on. The early smiths who produced such jewellery were obviously good hammer men, but otherwise technically limited.

New forms which appeared after about 800 B.C. were technically much advanced, involving the creation and bending of graduated gold tube, the production of cup shapes, and soldering. Dress fasteners, evolved from the torcs, were made from U-shaped tube with attached terminals. Some found at Morah in Cornwall end in open cups like trumpet bells, and those from the Bexley hoard in flat-topped knobs. Smaller versions of the Morah pieces were used as sleeve fasteners, anticipating the modern cufflink. An unusual form of jewellery from this period is the tress ring, a little penannular clasp to keep hair in a pony-tail. The Upton Barrow and Upton Level finds from Wiltshire were all thin gold sheathings made between 1650 and 1400 B.C. and intended mainly for covering buttons.

The Celts revolutionised British goldwork. Diodorus wrote of them: 'They accumulate large quantities of gold and make use of it for personal adornment, not only the women but also the men. For they wear bracelets on wrists and arms, and round their necks thick rings of solid gold, and they wear also fine finger-rings and even gold tunics.' This makes one wonder if in fact the Mold cape was not Celtic rather than British work. Irish legends confirm this Roman account of these gold-loving people with flowing yellow

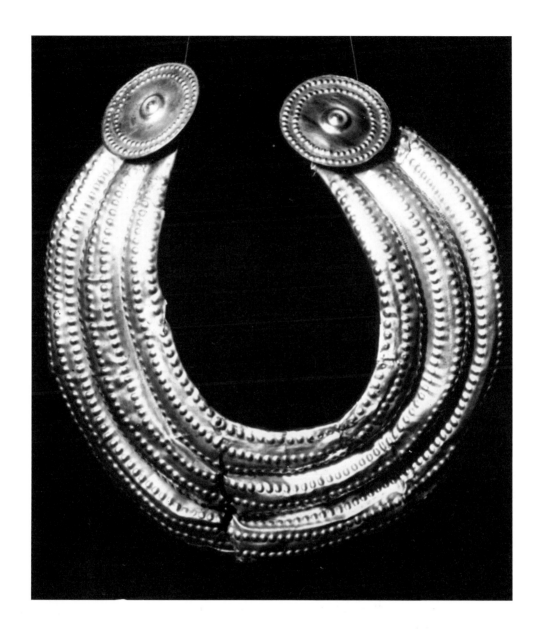

Irish torc made between 1000 and 500 B.C. *National Museum, Dublin.*

hair. The story of King Eochaid's wooing of Etain tells of her sitting by a spring 'washing her hair in a silver bowl with four golden birds on it . . . Wonderful ornaments of gold and silver with twining animal designs, in the tunic on her breast and her shoulders.' Another royal personage, Medb, travelled in the centre of a closely packed group of chariots so that 'no darkening might come to the golden diadem of the queen'.

Animal motifs endured in Celtic designs well into the Christian era. By the 8th century A.D. Ireland was the 'land of saints and scholars', where ecclesiastical city-settlements trained relays of missionaries to convert the barbarians on the Continent. Monastic art reached brilliant heights and smiths and jewellers enjoyed the most stimulating patronage. The church required illuminated gospels, covers, croziers, crosses, chalices, bells, shrines, reliquaries, censers, vestment brooches and many other devotional objects, providing native artists with a wide arena for their talents.

The Celtic Church was a sturdily independent body, sometimes to the point of offending the popes, and it developed largely in its own way. Since artist and cleric came of the same people, they shared the ethnic memory, and some strange echoes of the Celtic past appeared in this Christian art. Weird brutes, snakes, and dragons turn up continually, devouring or threatening little human figures in what Françoise Henry has called a 'universe of muffled anguish'. The snakes must have appeared during the Celts' early migrations, for there are none in Ireland. Or perhaps they are

Below: *electrum torc from the Snettisham treasure, 1st century* B.C., *with La Tene Celtic ornament on loop terminals. British Museum.* Right: *the Ardagh Chalice. National Museum, Dublin.*

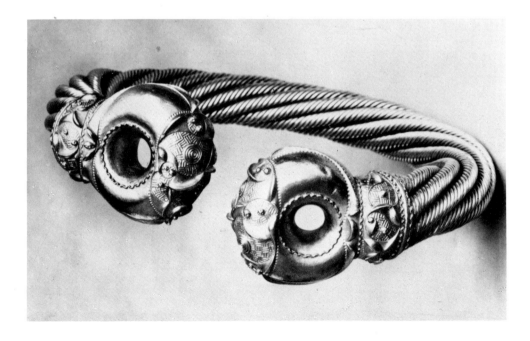

logical developments of the original spirals and convolutes, though this would not account for the other monsters.

Ireland's most prized examples of early Christian work are the Ardagh chalice, found in Limerick in 1868 by a peasant digging potatoes; the Tara brooch, discovered in a box near the mouth of the river Boyne; and the Cross of Cong. In none of these exquisite pieces is gold the body material; it is principally used in the extraordinary filigree work.

The chalice is in beaten silver, banded by gold filigree which is bossed with glass studs intricately cut into cross-shapes and glowing in rich reds, greens, blues and yellows. On the sides are four discs, each bearing a cross and decorated with studded filigree. On the handles are more tiny frames of filigree, the fine detail worked with incredible skill. Foot and bowl are joined by a stem of thick gilded bronze, on which the most complicated patterns of all are worked. Cut into the silver beneath the upper band are the names of the Apostles. The technical virtuosity of the whole cup, writes Mlle Henry, 'is such as to cause stupefaction'.

The Tara brooch is a cast silver ring of about 3.5 in diameter, with a long

Left: *the Shrine of St Patrick's Bell*. Right: *the Cross of Cong. National Museum, Dublin.*

pin stemming from a triangular top. The front of the ring is covered with tiny framed panels of gold filigree in which strange beasts and reptiles are formed of threads of fine tracery, with blue and red studs, and two small human heads in moulded glass. The back is decorated with glass studs in the same style as those on the chalice, and spirals so finely cut into the metal that there has been speculation whether this might not have been done with acid rather than with a tool. The Tara brooch was found with Scandinavian objects, which indicates that it had been looted by Viking raiders. Unfortunately, some of the wonderful filigree panels are missing.

The Cross of Cong, made for the High King of Ireland in 1123 as a shrine for a fragment of the True Cross, has the same blend of gold filigree animals and patterns, enamel and studs. Its central point is set with a large piece of quartz crystal, no doubt to draw the attention of the faithful when it was raised and caught the light. The inside of the cross is oak cased in copper, and the sides are covered in silver. For once the name of the artist is recorded:

Right: *an Irish gold collar made in about the 7th century* B.C. *It has cupped terminals and punched decoration. Victoria and Albert Museum, London.*

Above: *the Alfred Jewel, found at Athelney, Somerset, in 1693, has a figure in cloisonné enamel, set in a framework of filigree gold. English, 9th century. Ashmolean Museum, Oxford.*

Maelisu. It appears on the piece together with the names of the king and two bishops, but nobody knows what else this perfectionist craftsman may have made.

Much of the Irish Christian treasures disappeared with the rapacious Vikings, though the monks contrived an early warning system which enabled them to take refuge in their tall round towers on the sighting of the fearsome dragon ships. A crozier seized on one of these raids was discovered at Ekerö in Sweden and is now in the Stockholm museum. Otherwise little remains of one of the most productive periods of early Christian art, save for the matchless illuminated gospels.

Left: *the Sion Gospels. The cover is of beechwood overlaid with gold and enriched with cloisonné enamels and precious stones. French or German, about 1000 A.D. The embossed figure of Christ and the surrounding foliage date from the late 12th century. Victoria and Albert Museum, London.*

The Gothic Vogue

Gothic was a revolutionary and sophisticated style of church architecture developed in central Europe halfway through the Middle Ages. Despite its name, there was nothing barbarian about it. A Gothic building is a delicate composition of decorative columns soaring up to pointed arches, and the medieval stone carvers further elaborated this romantic setting with monstrous gargoyles, placid saints, thick-set peasants and riots of stylised foliage. Colour was also an important element of the Gothic style, as anyone who has stood in the nave of Chartres cathedral and looked up at the glorious stained glass is well aware. From this architecture all other forms of Gothic art developed, and of these other artforms, goldsmithing was not the least important.

The goldsmiths were called upon to provide furnishings and ornaments for the exciting buildings. The monstrances they made were Gothic chapels in miniature. The Reliquary of St Galgano, now in the cathedral museum of Siena, is like a three-tiered golden wedding cake. Inside the arches are repoussé panels of religious scenes, separated by buttresses with saints standing in the niches. The spire is of chased panels with enamel inserts depicting holy women, and above this is a lantern in the form of a little chapel with a cross for a finial. Emeralds and rubies are scattered over the structure to add the essential Gothic touch of colour. Made in the 13th century, this work is squat and strong, with a lingering Byzantine flavour. Another beautiful monstrance, made in 1456 for St Lorenzo of Voghera and now in the Castello Sforzesco in Milan, shows how the Gothic style proceeded towards a new lightness. Here the soaring effect is emphasised by placing the little chapel, with its enamelled windows, flying buttresses and intricate spire, on a slender stem rising out of a spreading foot.

When the goldsmiths made chalices and crosses, however, they could not copy architecture quite so literally, but they invariably managed to turn a boss or a knob into one of these little chapels, using the arches to house saints. A 15th-century Venetian chalice in the Victoria and Albert Museum shows how the smiths adapted Gothic decoration to their own forms. The artist began this silver gilt piece with the bases of six columns, which he pierced for lightness. Above these rises a tree-like stem, with saintly figures leaning against the trunk. At the base of the bowl the tree branches out, and winged cherubim peep from the foliage.

This element of stylised naturalism, taken from the stone carvers for use in church gold, was employed in turn by the makers of secular jewellery. The Duke of Aumale in 1396 gave Isabella of France a wedding present of

Left: *the crown of Princess Blanche, a Gothic jeweller's version of the allegorical garden so often described in medieval poetry. Schatzkammer, Munich.* Above: *a French ring brooch of the 15th century. Victoria and Albert Museum, London.*

'un cercle de pierrerie fait à manière de jardins'. Even more like a garden was the bridal crown of Princess Blanche of England, the daughter of Henry IV. The royal fleur-de-lis, set with stones on long collets and scattered with pearls, spring up like flowers from the gay circlet below. There are no arches or saints here, yet this crown of 1402 is as Gothic as a cathedral. It is also feminine and fashionable, reminding us that the Gothic age was a very fashion-conscious period. Contemporary portraits reveal the queens of the Middle Ages as among history's most elegant women, with a great fondness for jewellery. Queen Jeanne d'Evreux, for example, had four crowns, 14 coronals, clasps, brooches, a coronation girdle, other belts, and tressons for her hair.

But the sumptuary laws of the Middle Ages, like the Roman prohibitions before them, restricted the wearing of jewellery to those of high rank. In Spain in 1380 only princesses and queens were allowed to wear gold, silver, precious stones or pearls, while in England a statute of Edward III banned even knights and their families from wearing gold brooches or jewellery set with stones.

Badges and chains of office, as worn today by civic dignitaries and officers of associations, developed from one of the most popular forms of Gothic jewellery, the ring brooch. This derived from Scottish and Irish brooches and was used, like the famous Tara brooch, to hold the plaid or cloak on the

Royal gold cup, decorated with champlevé enamel. It has been considerably altered and restored since it was made in the 14th century. British Museum.

shoulder. It is still part of the kilted dress of both lands and continues to be produced. Basically it was a circle of gold or silver with a pin hinged on to it, and later a catch was added. Ring brooches were given as gifts between Gothic lovers, and in the 14th century heart-shaped versions emerged. In the 15th, the centre of the ring was filled with enamelled scenes of trysting, the hunt or heraldic animals.

Heraldic brooches developed into badges. The Earl of Warwick's followers wore one showing a bear and a ragged staff; the Duke of Norfolk's retinue one with ostrich feathers below a crown. Next, the brooch-pictures became pendants or plaques, hung from chains, linked gold emblems, or were stitched on to a neckband. The English kings wore a collar with double-S motifs on it. In the 1960s and 1970s, with men again wearing pendants and amulets, a Gothic fashion with noble associations has been revived.

Though a good deal of Gothic church goldsmithing survives, very little domestic plate has come down to us. Fashion is one reason for this. Because kings and courtiers wanted their tableware to be in the style of their own day, old plate was melted down to provide new. With the rising cost of war, too, outmoded palace vessels were likely to be sacrificed for the purchase of munitions and the raising of armies, in the same way as the Greek leaders had to plunder their shrines for gold. Among the 14th-century wares that avoided such fates is one remarkable piece. It is a cup made for the Duc de Berri, gathered into the royal treasures of England, presented to a Spanish envoy, re-acquired in the last century, and now in the British Museum. Considerably altered in its travels, it is nevertheless a unique example of medieval basse-taille enamelling applied to raised gold. The rich reds and blues are reminiscent of stained glass. The figures on lid, body and stem – an old man hobbling on crutches among holy women crowned with nimbi – remind us how the artists of the great cathedrals mixed the sublime and the ugly to cause surprise and underline the frailties of the flesh.

A 15th-century banker in his counting house. Contemporary illustration.

The Goldsmiths of the Renaissance

As Italy moved towards the 15th century, the feeling was stirring in the West that man ought not to be subjugated to such a degree by his priests as he had been for centuries past. The reaction was to look to logic rather than prayer for solutions to the human dilemma. It was logic that was changing the world; in the discovery of new lands, the applications of new technology, and the invention of new aids and instruments which proved that many things once thought to be caused by miracles or inexplicable phenomena were simply a matter of scientific measurement.

All around the Italians was the logic of their classical past – the philosophies of Plato and Aristotle, the buildings of their Roman ancestors, the proportions of their ancient statuary. And these monuments seemed to contain the germ of a lost truth. By starting again from the best values of a rational past, a great new culture might be raised on a surer, tested base of clear thought. This rebirth was to be accomplished in the Renaissance, which was the dominant influence on European art and thinking for the next four centuries.

The new movement put down its roots in a superb and congenial setting. In 1252 a new piece of money had appeared and was soon the standard gold coin in Europe. It was the first gold florin, called after the powerful city-state which issued it : Florence. There control lay not with the priests but with the guilds, including the bankers. The Florentine middle class was prosperous, and very sophisticated for its time, as Boccaccio was to reveal in the *Decameron*. Petrarch, the first great humanist, was of Florence too. Later, Lorenzo the Magnificent was to lead the Medici family into becoming the foremost patrons of the Renaissance. And where the Medici led, the middle class followed. The result was a flowering of culture on a scale that had not been seen since the days of Pericles.

The links with the classical past soon grew tenuous, and what had begun as revivalism developed into an original and vital force. It was the epoch of the all-round scholar or artist foreseen by Petrarch, the 'universal mind'. There was little that Leonardo da Vinci could not find to absorb his multiple talents. Michelangelo was painter, poet and architect. And many of the other giants of art were goldsmiths as well.

The workshops of the goldsmiths were recognised training grounds for painters. Ghiberti, who boasted that he did everything better than any of his contemporaries, first worked in gold. Botticelli refined his visions of Greek mythology and Christian gospel at the smith's bench. Verocchio learned design and dexterity as a gold worker's apprentice. So did Donatello, Mantegna and others. So did Dürer, indentured to his goldsmith father, and his technique remained that of a miniaturist.

The jewels of the early Renaissance were actually sculptures, showing the same command of drawing and design and the same orderliness that we find in the larger works of this epoch. The jewellers had no classical pieces to inspire them, and they derived their ideas from architecture and statuary. Many of their brooches are tiny relief plaques. Gold and enamel figures stand under classical porches with Corinthian columns and mouldings; acanthus and wreaths luxuriate and scrolls form complex frames.

These jewels were technically and artistically superior to any before them; indeed the Renaissance has seemed to many to be the high point of man's achievement in art. But this assessment is a matter of taste rather than of fact, and to others there seems to be a very thin borderline between such ebullience and the overdone. Was not the sheer profusion of jewels worn then by men and women of rank also bordering on vulgarity?

One of Holbein's portraits of Henry VIII shows him wearing one of the gold collars fashionable during that period. It is set with enormous red spinels, known as balas rubies. There are more stones in gold mounts on the

---

Right: *French cup and cover of enamelled cagework, set with rubies and with a woman's head in jacinth on the top. Late 17th century.* Over page: *gold tazza from the first half of the 16th century. It is set with coins and decorated with enamel.*

Above left: *a pendant cross of gold enamelled and set with diamonds. German, about 1560.* Lower left: *the underside of an Italian ring of the Renaissance, set with smokey quartz and decorated with champlevé enamel.* Above right: *very large enamelled gold pendant, French, second half of the 16th century. It is set with rubies and has a scene in enamel depicting the Sacrifice of Isaac by Abraham.*

Left: *two French gold snuff-boxes. The top one is attributed to Pierre Ayme Joubert, and was made in Paris in 1744. It is decorated with champlevé enamel. The other one was made in Paris in 1776 by Joseph Etienne Blerzy, and is decorated with painted enamel.*

slashed sleeves of his coat, on his tunic, on his hat. His wives were similarly adorned. In another Holbein picture Anne of Cleves wears a golden choker set with gemstones and pearls and hung with a gold cross. Below this are long gold chains. Her décolletage is enriched with jewels and her head-dress is loaded down with a huge jewel on one side. It was the same in the other courts of Europe. The Spanish, with the new gold of their American conquests, were even more ostentatious.

Many new styles of ring were devised during the Renaissance, including some with hinged heads. Often these contained portraits; others, the legendary poison which the Borgias are supposed to have dropped lethal doses of into their enemies' wine. Signet rings were in vogue, and so were twin, or gimmel, rings with little cast chased hands that locked them together to symbolise fidelity. People in mourning wore gold skull rings.

Despite the effort to throw off the clerical yoke, religion continued to be a strong influence. Religious themes were worked on to brooches, mirrors, pendants and hat ornaments. Ladies hung little pendant prayer-books with golden covers from their belts. A mid-16th-century example in the Victoria

A pendant book case in heavily enamelled gold. South German, about 1600. Victoria and Albert Museum, London.

and Albert Museum must be one of the most over-decorated gold objects ever made. On one side the creation of Eve is depicted in a Garden of Eden filled with repoussé beasts, birds, flowers and foliage. All this is enclosed in a wreath, every space of which is covered with nymphs, flowers and scrolls in repoussé and enamel. The decoration on the reverse, showing nymphs surprised while bathing in a fountain, is so ornate that it beggars description.

Goldsmiths tried to improve on nature too. When rich women wore furs, some replaced the animal's head by a golden muzzle set with gemstones.' A portrait of Isotta Brembarti by Moroni shows her in a marten skin with one of these gold heads. It is chased all over, with cabochon rubies for eyes and pearls dangling from its ears.

Below left: *Italian Renaissance watch-case enamelled with flowers.* Below right: *a pendant almost identical to the famous Canning jewel.*

From about 1560, forms of jewellery became even more complex and fantastic. Solid designs gave way to open work. A writhing mass of arabesques provides a background to the figures in the crucifixion pendant of the Emperor Rudolph II, which is now in the Louvre. The Canning jewel, to be seen in the Victoria and Albert Museum, represents a merman clutching a scimitar and shield, his body a single huge baroque pearl. To the later Renaissance, too, belong the portrait pendants, cameos or low reliefs in enamelled gold. Their successors were the delicate miniature paintings by Nicholas Hilliard and his contemporaries, set in decorated golden frames.

The plate was as lavish as the jewellery. An inventory of Queen Elizabeth I's tableware included 30 large gold standing salts, one set with diamonds and another 'containing a clocke'. A famous salt by Cellini which he made for Francis I is in the Kunsthistorisches Museum in Vienna. Its reclining Venus and bearded Neptune leaning on his sea-horses are typical of the classical motifs revived at the time. Studying this elaborate piece, it seems a pity that Cellini's boasted prowess in amours somewhat overshadows his reputation as an artist. But the Renaissance, in Rome as elsewhere, lost the sense of values that had brought it into being. The creation of masterpieces did not prevent the spread of corruption or the abuse of privilege. The Reformation was already under way, and beyond it loomed the distant shadows of even mightier revolutions.

5

Navigators' Gold

The navigators and explorers of the 15th and 16th centuries made deeper immediate impacts on Western society than the astronauts of our own time, because they came back to report that there were vast new empires with enormous stocks of gold for the taking. Often they returned with the mild and puzzled representatives of the peoples who inhabited these far worlds, who were gaped at as we ourselves might stare at a man from another planet. But it was seldom long before interest shifted from the person to his country's gold.

'I saw', wrote Albrecht Dürer, 'these wonderful artful things, and I was astonished at the subtle genius of the people in foreign lands.' He was looking at the Aztec treasures which Cortés had sent to the King of Spain and which were being exhibited in Europe. Among them was the sun-wheel that Moctezuma had offered the Spaniards as they advanced upon Tenochtitlán. It was of gold sheet wrapped over a wooden frame a yard wide and it weighed 35 lb. In his accompanying despatch to the king, Cortés wrote: 'These besides their value are such and so marvellous, that for the sake of their novelty and strangeness, they have no price, nor is it possible that all the princes ever heard of in the world possessed such treasures.'

Another gift which Cortés received from the Mexican emperor was a dozen blowguns, 'the mouthpieces and extremities . . . bordered with gold, a span deep, as was also the middle, all beautifully worked. He gave me a pouch of gold net-work for the balls, which he told me he would give me also of gold.' But of all these and the other Aztec goldwares dutifully sent on to the Spanish court, not one single piece has survived. Nor is anything left of the Inca gold wares which Pizarro despatched from Peru, the careful inventories of which can still be seen in Seville.

We can only glimpse these splendours in references in contemporary diaries. Garcilaso de la Vega, the son of a Spanish captain and an Inca

Contemporary drawing showing Cortés receiving tribute from the Aztecs.

princess, described the gold artefacts and decorations of the palaces of Cuzco, capital of the Inca empire:

The walls were lined with gold plates and, in preparing the stone, they left niches and empty spaces in which they put all sorts of animal and human figures, birds or wild beasts . . . all of which were made of gold or silver . . . Imitation of nature was so consummate that they even produced the leaves and little plants that grow on walls. They also scattered here and there gold or silver lizards, butterflies, mice and snakes which were so well made and cunningly placed, that one had the impression of seeing them run about in all directions.

The imperial gardens too were scattered with gold. Among the flowers growing naturally 'others were reproduced in gold and silver'. There were 'all kinds of gold and silver animals in these gardens, rabbits, mice, lizards, snakes, butterflies, foxes and wild cats. Then there were birds set in the trees as though they were about to sing.' In the bathroom there were 'large gold and silver basins into which water flowed through pipes made of the same material'. All the tableware 'whether for the kitchen or the dining hall, was of solid gold'.

Each new Inca built and furnished his own palace, and after his death it was inhabited by his *pucarina*, his effigy wrought from gold. Other dwellers were golden figures of his spiritual guardians in the form of a hawk or a child. One of these child figures, part of Atahualpa's ransom, was so heavy that it had to be broken up before it could be carried.

More magnificent even than the palaces was the Temple of the Sun. The emperors believed, like the Egyptian kings, that the sun was their divine ancestor, and each tried to outdo his predecessor in the gifts he brought. A sun symbol of thick gold plate, 'a round face prolonged by rays and flames', dominated the temple. All four walls were covered 'from roof to floor with plate and slabs of gold'. At seed time and harvest time, Garcilaso recounted, the temple terraces were carpeted with artificial cornfields made entirely of gold, 'the clods . . . the stems, the leaves and the cobs'.

The Inca himself wore a gold crown with feathers and carried a golden sceptre. Pizarro said he wore a mantle 'of delicate little leaves of gold' so thickly attached that none of the woven backing was visible. As marks of rank, emperor and courtiers wore enormous gold ear spools.

And yet, despite these fantastic glories, the Inca and Aztec empires had existed for little more than two centuries when the Spaniards destroyed them. The arts of the goldsmith had, however, been practised in both Mexico and Peru long before the Incas or the Aztecs seized power. Two thousand years before this the Chavin Indians of Peru had been working in gold. Their first products were sheet wares. They put on them in repoussé the same images of the gods which riot over the remnants of their architecture in relief carving. They made crowns and diadems, necklaces and dress-plaques. These were decorated with human figures with serpents issuing from their mouths, or with hawks, or most frequently with a jaguar. The Chavins' was a religious art, and these motifs probably had a talismanic significance.

The most important finds of their work were made at Chongoyape, the first by children playing there in 1928. There was a golden flute, gold tweezers for removing facial hairs, a cup and jewellery including spool ear-rings of the same type as the Incas wore. These objects are believed to date from about 400 B.C. The cup is chased with a double-headed serpent, and it shows that the Chavin goldsmiths were capable of soldering, raising vessels, possibly over a wooden former, and of making gold tube, probably by folding. They could also make hollow figures and beads, as well as pieces in multi-coloured gold which may have been produced by hot-hammering white and yellow gold together to weld them.

In Mexico the Mixtecs, the most skilful goldsmiths of the New World, had been working gold for 500 years. They used a technique called false filigree in which, instead of applying wires to the gold surface, they carved the pattern and cast it by a lost-wax process. The 'Pectoral of the Universe' in the Museo de Oaxaca consists of a series of lost-wax cast plaques joined by

Below: *Peruvian gold ceremonial vessel in the form of a dove. 12th- or 13th-century Chimu. Collection of Senor Mujica Gallo, Lima.*

Right: *Mexican pectoral representing Mictlan-Tecutli, god of darkness and of death. It was made by Mixtec goldsmiths between about* A.D. *1300 and 1450, and was found at Oaxaca.*

Above: *typical Ashanti gold ornaments made from sheet and repoussé chased. Probably made in the 19th century. British Museum.*

rings. The top one shows a kind of celestial ball-game symbolising the planetary motions (astronomy was highly developed in pre-Columbian America). Next comes a sun disc, then a moon plaque, and finally an earth plaque on which there is a fanged monster with a forked tongue. A fringe of gold feathers hangs below, and dangling from them are the little bells often found on Mixtec jewellery.

These goldsmiths had their own god, Xipe-Totec. He appears on a beautiful cast-filigree ring which is now in the Museum of the American Indian in New York. Two of the tiny bells hang from his ears. In the Museo Nacional in Mexico City there is a tiny gold skull, again with a bell. As the wearer moved, the jaws of the skull would open and close and the bell would tinkle. This Mixtec ability to make articulated cast jewellery impressed Spanish missionaries, one of whom saw a cast bird 'with a movable head, tongue and feet'.

Only one gold Mixtec mask survives. It is of Xipe-Totec himself, with large ear-rings and a butterfly nose ornament. Drawn across his face is a human skin. It was a reminder perhaps that anyone caught stealing gold from the smiths was flayed alive.

The Spanish empire, of course, was not the only one to emerge from the navigators' discoveries and the opening of new trade routes. The Portuguese and the British were expanding their possessions too, and gold was flowing into Europe from Africa and Asia as well.

A large showcase in the British Museum is filled with Ashanti work:

Left: *Peruvian vase, 12th–13th century* A.D., *set with turquoises. The crowned heads of various gods appear on the sides, and there is a frog on the base. Collection of Senor Mujica Gallo, Lima.*

repoussé discs, incredibly fine filigree, ceremonial objects, little nut-like bells and huge open-work rings. To many people the existence of a sophisticated gold culture in central Africa comes as a surprise, but there has been a strong metal-working tradition in this area from early times. The Nigerians were producing magnificent bronze portrait busts in the 11th century. Their little bronze animals, used to weigh out the gold grains and nuggets for foreign traders, are triumphs of skill and fantasy. With the alluvial gold of the river Niger so abundantly available to them, they and the metal-workers of Ghana and the Ivory Coast were bound to exploit its artistic possibilities.

Perhaps the most remarkable pieces from Africa are the filigree discs, which at first sight look like chased wares. On closer inspection they prove to consist of wire drawn to the fineness of a hair and enclosed in a frame. Two other pieces, apparently repoussé hedgehogs, turn out to be filigree master-pieces, made from the finest of wire soldered on a base. The chasing on this collection is also very accomplished, and the African smiths obviously were

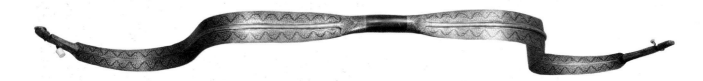

Above: *Kamar ceremonial bow with inlaid decoration.* Right: *dish in enamelled gold from Jaipur. Victoria and Albert Museum, London.*

masters of lost-wax casting as well, by which they made the little gold animal and plant ornaments for hairpins and the like.

Intricate filigree occurs only rarely in the gifted repertoire of the jewellers of India. Statuary made there earlier than 3000 B.C. shows that head-dresses, necklaces and bracelets were being produced and worn. Gold was certainly used in these, mostly in the form of beads, and plates.

Later jewellery, however, was predominantly composed of the rubies, emeralds, diamonds and pearls with which India was so richly endowed. In these pieces gold played only a supporting role to the splendid gemstones, and silver filigree was far more often employed. Considering the wealth of the Indian nobles and the value of the superb stones, the use of silver settings must have been a matter of preference rather than of limitation.

The Indian smiths also made fine quality gold chains, and what they could turn out in the way of gold filigree when given the opportunity may be judged from a casket exhibited in London in 1970. It came from Goa and is

believed to have been made in the 16th century. It consists of panels of filigree rondels not unlike later Ashanti work. The clasp is a cast-chased crocodile. The hinges and the finial on the bow-shaped carrying handle are in fleur-de-lis form, which suggests European influence, probably Portuguese.

Of Indian religious goldsmithing, one of the most sophisticated examples is a Buddhist reliquary from the Punjab, of the 2nd or 3rd century. It depicts

Left: *Burmese reliquary in gold, set with 38 rubies and one emerald, discovered in levelling a Buddhist temple at Rangoon, Burma, in 1855. It probably dates from the 15th century.* Above: *ceremonial water bowl, repoussé and chased, depicting the signs of the zodiac. From early 15th-century Burma.* Right: *a gold plaque with inscription in Burmese, ornamented with rubies. The ends are foliated and set with nine-stone ornament. Victoria and Albert Museum, London.*

repoussé figures under arches and is enriched with cabochon gemstones in box settings. Were it not for the Eastern character of the figures it could be mistaken for Byzantine. A reliquary is also part of an important find which illuminates the history of the goldsmith in Burma. It is like a large bell, decorated with courses of cast-chased and chased work, and at the top is a screw thread to which a tall finial was attached. This piece was found in 1855 on the site of an old pagoda together with a gold bowl and a votive helmet set with gemstones around the chased rim. From this evidence, highly skilled goldsmiths were working in Rangoon in the second half of the 15th century.

The Chinese worked in gold from a fairly early period. Their modelling, engraving, chasing and piercing is of high quality, and their later enamel work has the subtlety of colouring which made Chinese ceramics so renowned. Birds, phoenixes and the familiar dragons are the motifs of jewellery which has been preserved. A characteristic form was the filigree plaque, combining repoussé and pierced work in a web of golden tracery. On a 15th-century example in the British Museum, two dragons romp within a frame of uncut stones in box settings. The phoenixes were produced as early as the 10th or 11th century and as late as the brink of modern times. One on a fine early hair ornament has chased feathers on a three-dimensional body, a head with pierced cresting, and a fan tail set with pearls. It is from the Sung dynasty and is now in a Swedish private collection.

A Sung gold plate in the Victoria and Albert Museum indicates the luxury of the imperial table as well as the smith's finesse. It is hammered up from sheet, the centre being engraved with a lotus flower and leaf, beautifully composed within a band of chasing done with a matting punch. The rim has a chased motif of leaves forming rondels on a matted background. Compared with the quantity of lovely jades, ceramics and bronzes that still exist, however, regrettably few Chinese gold wares have survived.

Though the Portuguese developed big gold deposits in Africa and Brazil,

A chased and engraved dish made in China probably during the Sung dynasty. Victoria and Albert Museum, London.

they found little or none when they landed in Japan in 1542. Examples of early Japanese goldsmithing are very rare indeed, and what does survive is very similar to Chinese work. Although the primitive Japanese religion was based on worship of a sun-goddess and the imperial family believed themselves to be descended from her, it was not until a few years ago that this people began to show much interest in gold or gemstones. In this, Japan is unique among the major nations. At last, however, the Japanese seem to be developing a distinctive style in jewellery design which has already been very successful in international competitions. And many people believe that this new wave of Japanese artists will have an increasing influence on the world's jewellery in the next decade.

6

Gold Work of the 17th, 18th, and 19th Centuries

From the 17th century onwards there was a great change in the way people displayed the gold they owned. The showy excesses of the late Renaissance were a thing of the past. Instead of being hung about the person in profusion, gold was now used for an increasing range of intimate little objects which were more or less practical and functional. This in no way curbed the gold-smiths' imaginative fancies. Indeed, the popularity of innovations such as the watch and the snuff box gave them new opportunities to produce work of grace and elegance.

The 17th century was an age of gardens, and its passion for them is reflected in much of its art. Elegant parks and pleasure grounds were laid out; flowers and bowers were endlessly evoked in poetry and song, depicted in fashionable embroideries and on all manner of personal and household belongings. The flower style was propagated in France through the publica-tion of engravings by Gilles Légaré, Heinrich Raab, and other designers. Their delicate but lively floral motifs were soon being applied to jewellery. An especial favourite was the tulip, a shapely newcomer first grown in Europe in 1559. For a while this addiction reached such a height that it was known as 'tulipomania'. Even the pea-pod was adopted as a decorative pattern, giving rise to the style of jewellery called *cosse de pois*.

Above: *a 17th-century goldsmith's workshop. A modern craft workshop looks almost exactly like this.*

Right: *Queen Anne cup and cover, 6 inches high, made by Pierre Harache. It fetched £31,000 ($71,400) in London in 1967. Over page: Regency banqueting plate supplied by Rundell, Bridge and Rundell to the first Earl of Harewood between 1812 and 1815. The large centre tray was by Digby Scott and Benjamin Smith, the rest by Paul Storr. It was sold for £44,300 ($106,300) in London in 1965.*

The flower vogue led to an outburst of colour in jewellery, which coincided with new techniques of applying it. At first, during the early part of the century, colour was little more than an accent in the arabesque-like patterns on cases for watches and miniatures. Petals and leaves, done in champlevé, would show up as rich splashes against the golden background. Gradually the balance was reversed, until enamel work covered the entire surface or left only highlights of bare metal. A refinement of the trend was the beguiling art of enamel painting, the invention of which is attributed to Jean Toutin. A layer of white enamel is laid and fired on to the gold surface, and the miniature is then carried out in coloured enamels. Geneva became a centre of enamel painting, with a renowned school founded by Jean Petitot and the Huaud family.

The gold look was now out of vogue for jewellery too as a result of improvements in gem cutting. The well cut stone, with its many facets, now scintillated as it had never done before. Rings, brooches and necklaces were designed to focus attention on the gems. Often the only gold visible from the front was the tips of the claws or the bezel in which a stone was set.

Gold undisguised though was used for many of the other fashionable personal ornaments of this period. Chief among these was the gold watch, which still retains to this day some of the prestige it enjoyed in the 17th and 18th centuries. By the end of the 17th century, with the invention of the balance spring and the great improvements in wheel cutting machinery, the watch was a reliable timekeeper. The watch movements, produced by craftsmen like Thomas Tompion in the 17th century and their successors in the 18th, were so expensive and so highly regarded that they were frequently protected by a double case, the pair-case, and sometimes even by three cases. The inner case was often of plain gold. Round this went another gold case, usually repoussé chased with a scene from classical mythology. These fine examples of goldsmithing, made by specialist jewellers, were sometimes in their turn protected by an outer casing of leather.

Watches were worn hanging from gold chatelaines of repoussé plaques with further mythological imagery on them. Up to about 1770 the European gentleman's fob watch had mixed classical and rococo decoration, then the style changed. Later chatelaines were of painted enamelled plaques joined by lengths of fancy gold chain. By the 19th century the making of watch cases as well as movements had been industrialised to meet demand, and the standard gold watch was a rather mundane article as far as men's timepieces went, though elaborately hand-worked specimens were still produced by a

---

Left: *a set of Flemish gold plaques, made in the first half of the 16th century, but mounted in a later setting.*

Above left: *chatelaine from Sir Chester Beatty's collection, decorated with coloured gold appliqué*. Above right: *a gold 'nécessaire', made in England about 1750.*

few houses. Women's watches of the period were far more interesting and varied. They were pinned on blouses and dresses as gold and enamelled pendants in the form of mandolins, harps, fruit, eggs, butterflies, flower baskets, and even barometers. These fanciful cases housed a small movement and a tiny dial. Side by side with these, watches of more usual form were produced, decorated with all-over enamel paintings often contained within

A heavy gold pocket watch, with dials on both sides of the case, made by Perolia in 1750.

a circle of half-pearls. The subjects of the enamel painting included the popular flower motifs, allegories such as Peace returning with Abundance (after the Napoleonic wars), and biblical scenes, such as Susanna and the Elders.

A later 19th-century vogue was the *sous fondant* style, which combined enamel work and chasing in some of the prettiest watches of the time. A Geneva watch from the house of Doehner has a painted enamel centrepiece on the back, with roses and other flowers in a wreath of blue vine leaves. The rest is covered with matted chased decoration that provides a soft background of yellow gold. The same kind of contrast was obtained by masking portions of the case during enamelling. A charming watch in the Geneva Museum has a little Swiss landscape by the enamel painter Rosselet in the centre, surrounded by a golden wreath on an area of deep blue enamel, with gold vine leaves enclosing the whole.

The 19th-century man's watch was seldom carried without its chain. Those who could afford them wore heavy gold links across their velvet waistcoats, in many cases with a golden key, signet or medal also attached. A lighter variant was the gold albert, so called after Queen Victoria's consort, which hung from a bar in the lapel buttonhole to the breast pocket where the watch was kept. By the first quarter of the 20th century, however, the gold pocket or fob watch and all its trappings was giving way to the wrist watch of our own day. And with it passed a vehicle for a fascinating form of art in miniature.

Small boxes and containers of many kinds were essential equipment among people of position in the 17th and 18th centuries. There was the pomander, with several little compartments like the segments of an orange, filled with perfume and fragrant substances to ward off the smells of the cities. Some of these were delightful and intricate examples of the small-worker's skill. Pendants included slender, beguiling cases bearing a miniature portrait of the wearer or perhaps the donor. Inside there may have been a love token, a keepsake or a verse. Then there was the succade, a box for digestives, holding dried or sugared fruits 'to fortify the stomack'. Patch boxes were first made at about the same time. They contained tiny stars, crescents and spots of gummed taffeta, beauty aids whose precise placing on face and body was a minor art in itself. On their chatelaines women carried etuis, the long oval cases which held their needles and sewing aids.

But the most important of all was the snuff box. The snuff habit came from America along with the Indian gold, for the inhabitants had shown their conquerors how to powder tobacco and sniff it up the nostrils. They would have been bewildered to see the foppish etiquette which European gallants devised for it. In the way he took snuff, wrote an 18th-century commentator, 'a man's background and upbringing were laid bare'. Clues to his taste and wealth were divined both from the quality of his snuff box and the flourishes with which he plied it.

The earliest snuff accoutrements consisted of a rasp for grating the tobacco and a leather-covered flask to put it in, a small-scale copy of a musketeer's powder flask. By the end of the 17th century elegant hinged boxes had been evolved, and gradually the area around the Place Dauphine in Paris became crowded with the workshops of goldsmiths specialising in their manufacture. This area is still known as the Quai des Orfèvres.

The box-makers had their problems and so did their clients. Louis XIV hated snuff, and also there were now harsh sumptuary laws in France to restrict the ownership of gold. Under an edict of 1700 no more than an ounce of it was allowed to be used in any one object, and tortoise-shell came into

An 18th-century round gold snuff-box.

---

fashion as an alternative, embellished with splendid gold piqué work. Malachite boxes were another substitute, enclosed in complex cages of chased gold. From this expedient the so-called cage style developed. But what the French courtiers could not buy at home they imported or smuggled, and in 1721 the manufacture of all-gold boxes was permitted again, with a limit of seven ounces of 20.25 carats fineness per box. From then until the French Revolution the box-makers thrived.

French boxes are in many styles. They are oval, square or oblong. Some have two compartments with separate lids, others are ornate fantasies like the golden coach in the Wallace Collection. They were decorated with masks, shells, birds, beasts, strapwork patterns, Chinese and Indian designs, architectural motifs, and enamel paintings in the manner of Watteau, Fragonard and Boucher.

English boxes rival the French in quality, though their decoration tends to be more subdued. Repoussé mythological scenes similar to those on watch

An early 18th-century French snuff-box, in which the jeweller has made the most of the gold he was legally allowed to use by creating a delicate cagework to enclose an agate box.

cases were the most popular subjects in the early 18th century. After some flirtation with rococo, the English makers adopted the neo-classical style. The German, Russian, Swiss and Dutch makers followed French models, but their work rarely had the same grace and elegance.

The goldsmiths of the 18th century also devised boxes for other purposes. There was the vinaigrette, from which aromatic vinegars of cloves, lemon, quince, bergamot and wormwood were sniffed through a grille under the lid to dispel the 'vapours'. Cosmetic boxes, holding rouge and salves, sometimes had a small mirror in the lid like a modern compact, and other miniature toilet boxes held a little sponge or a scrap of soap. There were little nutmeg graters with their own rasps, most of them in silver rather than gold, and gold toothpick boxes. An English pick box, presented to Warren Hastings by a group of Indian maharajahs, has an enamel portrait of him in a blue surround, its lid edged with half-pearls.

Box-making goes on up to the present day in London, Paris, Geneva and

Gold box presented to Queen Elizabeth the Queen Mother by the Fishmongers' Company. It was made by Gerald Benney.

New York. Lids and bases fit snugly together, the hinges are all but invisible and the clasps are tiny masterpieces of engineering. Engine-turned and textured decoration gives them a 20th-century flavour, but they are as beautifully fashioned as those designed by Jean Bourget and Meissonnier for the courtiers of France.

In so far as one can date such things, the Romantic Revolution began in the 1780s. The effect of this revolution was to send the designers of the applied arts, the jewellers among them, on a ceaseless quest for novelty in the lumber rooms of the past. It created, too, an interest in lands far removed from Europe, to which distance lent enchantment. The jewellers borrowed their motifs from the Gothic, from the Renaissance, from the Classical world, from the Etruscans, from the Egyptians and from the Moors. The Romantic Revolution led also to a new interest in the flora and fauna of the countryside, the frontiers of which were being pushed back by the urban sprawls and the dark satanic mills which were the by-products of another and uglier revolution. Rousseau had sent the artists 'back to nature', and the jewellers of the late 18th and the 19th centuries endeavoured to reproduce faithfully the flowers and the birds, lizards, butterflies and dragonflies in gold and gemstones.

France had been the hub of European goldsmithing since the Thirty Years' War, and after the Revolutionary period of austerity she became once

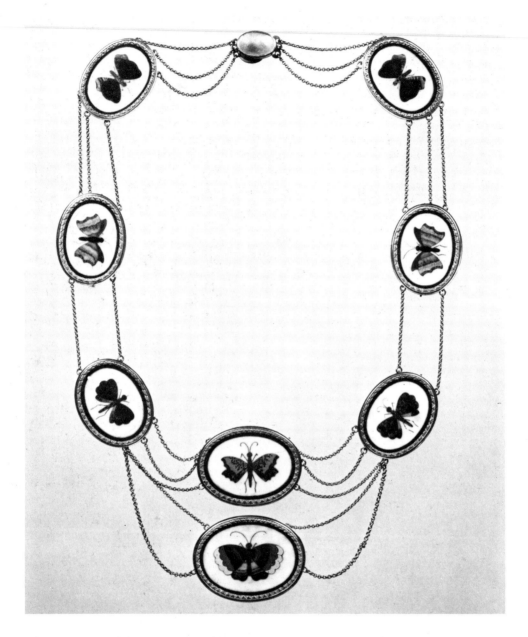

Above: *an early 19th-century gold and enamelled necklace showing the static quality of romantic naturalism. Victoria and Albert Museum, London.*

Right: *the Armada Jewel, given by Queen Elizabeth I to Sir Thomas Heneage. It was possibly painted by Nicholas Hilliard. Victoria and Albert Museum, London.*

again the centre of fashion. The Empire style went hand-in-hand with a vogue for pseudo-Greek jewellery. In David's painting of the coronation of Napoleon, the women of the court wear Greek-type diadems, or gold wreaths,

Right: *a scent bottle in the shape of a dog. The animal is quite realistic, if rather lifeless, and has a second very small dog sitting between its front paws. English, 1750. Below: a memorandum book made in Paris in 1761. It has panels of Japanese lacquer mounted in chased gold. Victoria and Albert Museum, London.*

Left: *rococo Dutch gold cup and cover, 13 inches high, made at The Hague in 1743. It was sold in London in 1970 for £7,000 ($16,800).*

round their brows. A more mawkish revival was the epidemic of Gothic in the 1840s, the jewellers' least happy love affair with the past. Their brooches in *style cathédrale* were highly romanticised visions of an era which the 19th century did not really understand. Insipid angels floated improbably in diaphanous gowns, and couples mooned vapidly under arches. The vigour and earthiness of the medieval originals was completely lacking.

To make it easier for British jewellers to produce in quantity for their

Above: *gold bracelet designed by Pugin in 19th-century Gothic style and decorated with enamel and half pearls. Victoria and Albert Museum, London. Opposite, left: a typical Victorian brooch decorated with enamel and set with diamonds. Centre: a Victorian gold brooch set with coral. Right: a late Victorian gold brooch.*

growing middle class clientele, the nine-carat standard was legalised in 1854, though many people contended that something containing only 0.375 gold could not properly be termed a ware of gold. Nevertheless, since then the majority of Britain's gold products have been made to this standard. Low as it is, it was frequently not maintained in the second half of the century, and dealers who offer non-hallmarked items of this period for sale in the United Kingdom risk prosecution for dealing in sub-standard gold.

The industrial revolution was bound to apply to jewellery as well as to other things for which there was increasing demand, and factories were started in Birmingham in the 18th century. The best known was Matthew Boulton's at Soho Hill. France and the rest of Europe followed these examples, and soon mass-produced pieces stamped out of gold or base metal were available to everybody. In Germany, America and Britain mile upon mile of gold chain poured from ingenious new machines each day. Two or three men could look after them in the workshop and collect the lengths of chain for soldering to bracelets and brooches, or for weaving into entire purses and handbags. Gold no longer belonged to the few, but to the millions. Everyone wanted to own something golden, no matter how trifling or tawdry it might be.

Compared with the deluge of jewellery, gold tablewares were produced only very occasionally from the end of the 16th century onward. In England

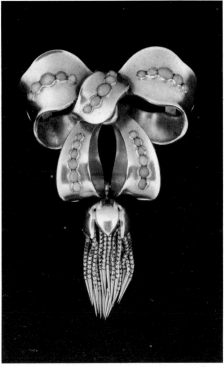
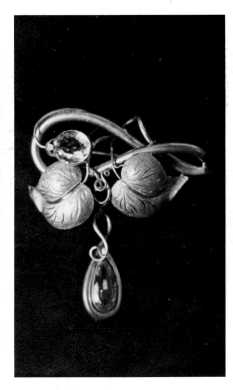

the Civil War brought a clean break with the sumptuous past, and accumulated treasures were melted down to pay for powder and shot. The great livery companies were forced to sell their plate when Charles I levied a loan of £120,000 on the City of London. Private citizens were similarly levied, and the king sent his wife to the Continent to pawn the royal jewels. Cromwell's contempt for 'baubles' led to the destruction of even more of the treasures of Renaissance England.

When the Commonwealth came to an end, the Renaissance style had all but disappeared, a memory of it lingering only in the restrained ornament on Caroline cups, tankards and bowls. The measure of the change is to be seen in the work which Charles II and his court commissioned in the years

Peasant jewellery of the early 19th century; left: *Spanish,* right: *Flemish.*

following the Restoration. The vessels are eminently practical, almost puritanical in their forthrightness. A two-handled cup and cover, sold in 1970, illustrates this new plainness. It was made as a drinking cup for caudle, a nourishing gruel taken by women in childbed. The piece is sumptuous only because it is in gold. The handles are like branches of acanthus without leaves, and the only unnecessary ornamentation is the elaboration of the ring handle on the lid into a serpent.

There were few goldsmiths left to serve the returned court. During the war and the Commonwealth they had been forced to find other occupations, and no apprentices had been trained. It was not until the last quarter of the 17th century that Huguenot smiths, taking refuge from religious persecution in France, laid the foundations of a great age of goldsmithing. They were among the most skilled metalworkers the world has ever seen, conceiving and executing subtly beautiful forms. They initiated the great epoch of English silverware in the early 1700s, and when they worked in gold, as they sometimes did, their work seemed even more inspired.

To begin with, the Huguenot smiths introduced into England a baroque style which they had evolved on the Continent. The silversmith Pierre Platel produced two outstanding examples of late baroque work in the gold ewer and basin commissioned by the first Earl of Devonshire and completed in 1701. These pieces, still in the possession of the Devonshire family, are on loan to the Victoria and Albert Museum and can be seen in the Jewel Room. They show that gold vessels have a richness and a solidity quite different from the cool beauty of similar vessels in silver. One can sense the weight of the ewer without even touching it.

The Queen Anne period saw the classical forms denuded of baroque ornament. This early 18th-century English work has been called 'plain', but handsome is more appropriate. The curves of the baluster shapes need no ornamentation. A Pierre Harache cup and cover made in this style are as logically composed as a Bach fugue.

This plain fashion was followed by a riotous style, the Rococo, which became fashionable in England in the 1740s. 'Rococo' derives from *rocaille*, meaning rock-like, but all this style had in common with rocks was its characteristic asymmetry. Rococo motifs were opulent and varied – shells, scrolls, masks, flowers, sea-creatures and chinoiserie. Outside France, only Paul de Lamerie, the great English smith of Huguenot descent, really accomplished much with this idiom. In the hands of lesser artists it lost its delicacy and liveliness, and it is for this reason perhaps that the style was so short-lived.

The Rococo period was followed in England by the age of the Adam brothers, a period of Classical revivalism inspired by the discoveries of the remains of Roman cities in Italy. Then came the great derivative age of the 19th century. All the diverse elements of 19th-century art, except the Gothic, are present in the monumental gold banqueting suite supplied by Rundell, Bridge and Rundell to the first Earl of Harewood between 1812 and 1815. This was the work of the great Regency silversmith Paul Storr, with the exception of one large tray which was designed by Digby Scott and Benjamin Smith.

This plate was not primarily made for use, but for show. The massive centrepiece recalls the Baroque, with classical touches. Three Roman matrons hold laurel wreaths while the central column develops into an exotic pineapple. Honeysuckle, a motif inspired by decorations found at Pompeii, mingles with acanthus foliage on the branches above. On the finial dish, twisting vines evoke the Classical Bacchanalia and the naturalism of the Romantic period. Supporting this golden display are four seated bears, which represent two periods. The crested shields they hold suggest medieval heraldry, but they are also well observed animals in the Romantic style of Landseer's paintings. The candelabra are entirely baroque; the vases of the

A rococo bowl, perhaps of Batavian origin, made about 1750. It was sold in London in 1970 for £1,150.

suite derive their form from Pompeii pottery; the ornate baskets have feet in the shape of Egyptian winged figures.

No great quantity of gold plate was made in the 19th century, but what was tended to be in this monumental vein. Storr was one of the finest smiths in history, and the Harewood plate is at once the typical and the greatest example of European goldsmithing on the large scale from Napoleonic to Victorian times.

7

Gold Trends of Our Own Times

By the 1890s, the Romantic Revolution had run its course. The ideas that had seemed new and vital a century earlier had long ago become spiritless clichés mindlessly repeated. Change had appeared inevitable for more than a decade, but it was slow in coming. To some enlightened people, like William Morris, it seemed as though they were living in a cultural vacuum. They preached beauty and functionalism and the values of individual craftsmanship, but the world seemed deaf to truth. The materialistic age thundered on, and the factories continued to produce only ugliness and mediocrity. Then quite suddenly a new art was born – Art Nouveau.

The practitioners of the Art Nouveau returned again to nature, as the Romantic artists had done at the beginning of the 19th century. From nature the Art Nouveau school, however, distilled new and sensuous forms. Their flowers and animals were lively and vigorous as the naturalism of the romantics had never been. Their colour schemes were soft and subtle, influenced by the work of the Impressionist and Post-Impressionist painters. Their muted blues and greens were like those in a Paul Cézanne watercolour.

The most effective of all the creations of the age of Art Nouveau was the jewellery. The artists who created it turned their backs on the idea of jewellery as a form of portable wealth. They were more concerned with artistic than with intrinsic values. They did use gold, though they also used iron when it suited their purpose, but they disliked the opulence of brilliant and expensive gemstones geometrically faceted. They preferred the opaque and less expensive gem materials, mother of pearl, opal, amber and ivory, and they used the baroque pearls that had fascinated the designers of the

Renaissance. The men who composed lilies into a writing composition expressing the growth rhythms of nature, whose bright lizards seemed to crawl across a glove or a bodice, who anticipated Surrealism by enclosing a woman's face within the frail wings of a butterfly, were different in another way from the jewellers of the earlier decades of the century. The 19th-century jewellers were for the most part anonymous craftsmen. The creators of the Art Nouveau jewellery were artists, personalities whose names were linked with what they produced.

The most important of these was René Lalique. He had studied art in London and Paris and was apprenticed to the goldsmith, Louis Aucoc.

Above: *a gold and enamelled brooch by Art Nouveau artist and jeweller Georges Fouquet. Victoria and Albert Museum, London.*

Right: *Nautilus cup, mounted in gold and set with onyx, chalcedony and paste intaglios. The cup was made in Warsaw in 1770 for King Stanislas August of Poland by his court jeweller, Jean Martin. Victoria and Albert Museum, London. Over page: two pieces of jewellery by René Lalique, made in about 1900. Musée des Arts Décoratifs, Paris.*

Above: *three-coloured gold egg made by Carl Fabergé for Tsar Nicholas II to present to the dowager Empress Marie Feodorovna in 1895.*

Gold necklace set with diamonds, pearls and tektites (extraterrestrial stones). It was made by the Swiss designer Gilbert Albert.

Though he opened his own *atelier* in 1881, it was not for another 10 years that Lalique became an important name. It was then that he made a parure, a matched set of jewellery, for the actress Sarah Bernhardt, who became a great patron of the Art Nouveau jewellers and helped to get their work known in the world of fashion. Lalique seems to have favoured enclosed designs. A necklace of his, in the Musée des Arts Décoratifs in Paris, has a large plaque pendant with a rigid gold frame, inside which is a composition of diamond-set hazel nuts and enamelled leaves with big cabochon sapphires lurking in the spaces between.

For a time, the style had an international vogue. Art Nouveau designs were

Freer and more sensual than Lalique's creations were those of his Parisian contemporary, Georges Fouquet, who was also patronised by Bernhardt. He made a strange bracelet and ring for her from a design by Alphonse Mucha. The snake with its head of green champlevé enamel, coiling body and bright ruby eyes, has an evil quality quite unlike the tame creatures of the romantic period. This writhing, reptilian atmosphere is present in much Art Nouveau work.

For a time, the style had an international vogue. Art Nouveau designs were produced by Henri Vever in Paris, Philippe Wolfers in Belgium, and by Tiffany in New York. But the style degenerated rapidly. In retrospect it emerges as one of the most significant periods of goldsmithing in the history of the craft. Otherwise, however, little remained of it apart from daffodil dados and cast-iron fireplace ornaments, still to be seen in a few provincial

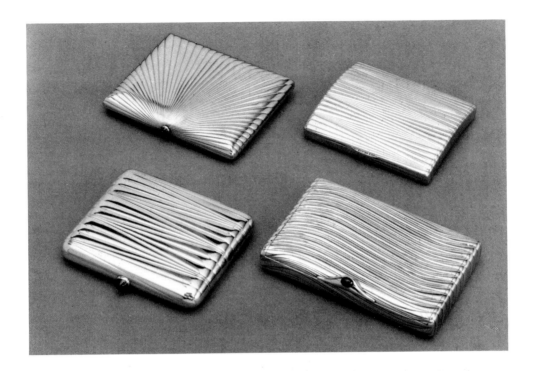

Far left: *Art Nouveau peacock pendant in gold, enamelled and set with diamonds. It was made by L. Gautriat. Victoria and Albert Museum, London.* Left: *Art Nouveau scent bottle by Tiffany and Company, with a gold hinged top in the form of a double headed lion.* Above: *four gold cigarette cases by Carl Fabergé. Those on the right are made from a combination of red and green gold.*

boarding houses, until the revival of interest in the style in the 1960s.

In Russia that gifted goldsmith Peter Carl Fabergé experimented with Art Nouveau ideas for a short time. Of Huguenot descent, he took control of his family's workshop in St Petersburg at the age of 24. Almost from the outset, Fabergé specialised in *objets d'art* rather than personal jewellery. His work won him the gold medal at the Pan-Russian Exhibition in 1882: then a collection of his pieces shown at the Paris Exhibition of 1900 brought him the Légion d'Honneur and made him the most famous goldsmith in Europe. Fabergé's mastery of technique has never been surpassed. He alloyed his gold to produce a whole range of colours from green to red, often combining them in the same piece, as the French box-makers had done in the 18th century. His transparent enamels, usually applied over engine-turned surfaces, were renowned for their clarity and variety. A sampler which hung in his workshop showed 144 different shades.

The best known Fabergé treasures are the surprise Easter eggs which he produced every year for Tsar Nicholas II to give to his family. Some are superb, like the 1897 egg which contained a tiny scale model of the coronation coach. But others, like the Lilies of the Valley egg for the dowager empress Maria Feodorovna, are rather trite and ostentatious. His less dazzling pieces are his happiest – the scent bottles, enamelled stick handles, boxes and bell pushes. The ribbed Fabergé cigarette cases with jewelled thumbpieces were the forerunners of designs which houses like Cartier and Asprey produced for their rich clients. The most charming of all his works, however, were his little bouquets, which recall the golden roses which the popes presented to heads of state in the 15th century.

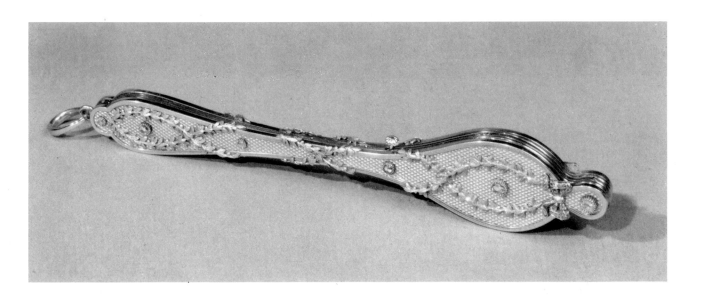

Left: a basket of lilies of the valley in yellow gold. The flowers have engraved green gold stalks, and grow in a bed of spun green gold 'moss'. Presented to the Tsarina by the Siberian iron section of a trade fair in 1896. Above: *red gold lorgnette enamelled in pale transparent mauve and overlaid with carved dull green gold trails of leaves and berries.*

There are two exquisite examples in the Royal Collection at Sandringham, a spray of japonica and a single carnation which stand in little pots cut from colourless quartz. The spray has a green gold stalk, carved nephrite leaves and gold flowers coloured with opaque enamels. In the centres of the flowers are rose-cut diamonds. The masterpiece of Fabergé flower pieces is the basket of lilies of the valley which the management of the Siberian iron works commissioned as a gift to the Tsarina Alexandra in 1896. The basket itself is woven from yellow gold sheet and wire. It is filled with moss, represented by spun green gold wire. The stalks of the lilies are in green gold, the leaves are again of nephrite, and the bells consist of pearls set with rose diamonds. Fabergé's workshops employed well over 100 men, but guiding them all was the genius of this great goldsmith.

The first 60 years of the present century was not a great period of goldsmithing. Gold clips, compacts, cigarette cases and holders, boxes, lighters and cuff links were produced in quantities never previously dreamed of. But, excellent though the workmanship often was, these pieces had little or no artistic merit. Mechanical decoration, like engine-turning, imparted a banal uniformity; even when made by individual craftsmen they still tended to look as though they came from a factory. Only a few jewellers paid any heed to the artistic modes which came and went, and ventures in originality like the cubist jewellery of Jean Fouquet and Raymond Templier were exceptional. Such art jewellery as was produced was no more successful than the Surrealist jewellery which Dali designed, or the attempts of Giorgio di Chirico to translate his own vision into gold. Artists who have not learned the skills of the craft seldom produce satisfying gold work.

Only in the 1960s did goldsmithing rise again to the status of an art form. And this revolution resulted not from artists turning to jewellery, but from jewellers turning to art. The new generation of designers came from the craft schools, young men and women who had been trained in the traditions and found them sterile. Typical of them is the fine Finnish smith Björn Weckstrom. He had wanted to be a sculptor, but he compromised with his parents' conservative attitude towards art as a career and enrolled at the goldsmiths' school in Helsinki. His reactions were like those of students all over Europe at the time.

'We were doing such ugly things', Weckstrom said afterwards. 'The forms were no longer fresh. The trade was screaming for a change, and it seemed to me so easy to change it.' Others who saw this need clearly were the Swiss designer Gilbert Albert, who was employed in the workshops of Patek Philippe, and Andrew Grima, who had inherited his father's traditional jewellery business. They were among the advance guard of the revolutionaries.

The new wave of artist-jewellers, as is the habit of new waves everywhere, despised the designs that had gone before them. In place of pretty flower brooches, faceted gemstones and the commercial slickness of polished gold, they evolved their own motifs – abstraction, texture and uncut crystals. Albert distils his rhythmical patterns from ideas he finds in nature. Weckstrom, walking or sailing at weekends, observes odd rock formations, boulders in a stream, a wind-curved sail. Grima, until recently borrowed more directly from nature, making gold castings from twigs, sticks of cinnamon, even fragments of Shredded Wheat.

The roughly-surfaced gold of modern jewellery is also a return to nature, a conviction that gold is never more beautiful than the way it looks when it is found. Much of Weckstrom's work looks like a series of nuggets strung together. The same idea runs through pieces by Louis Osman, the English designer who made the new crown for the Prince of Wales.

The new, fresh and vital insights of Tapio Wirkkala in Finland, Sigmund Persson in Norway, Friedrich Berker in Germany, John Donald in Britain, Yasuki Hiramatsu and Reiko Yamada in Japan and a score of other modern

Opposite page, above: *a ring called Spring Breeze, designed by Björn Weckstrom*. Below left: *An 18 carat gold decanter by modern British designer and craftsman Gerald Benney*. Below right: *pendant watch with rutilated quartz crystal over the dial, designed by Andrew Grima*.

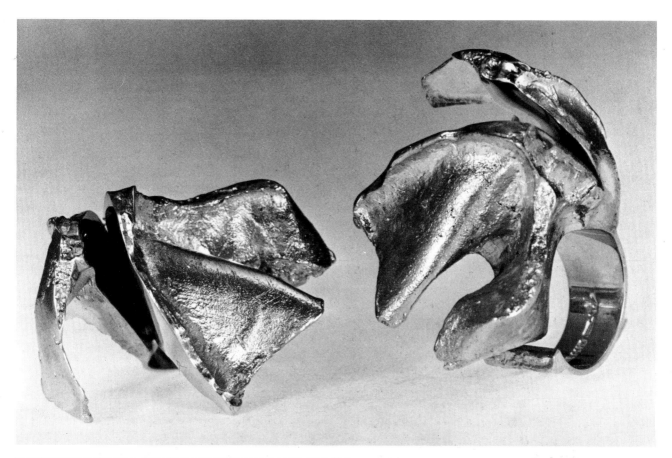

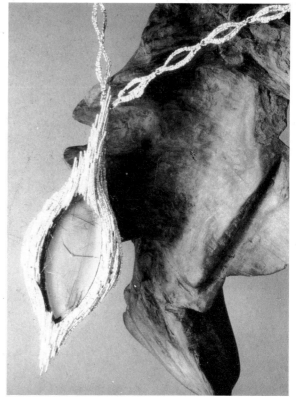

Left: *a 5 ft long necklace in 22 carat gold set with pearls, designed and made by Louis Osman. Above left: a goblet designed and made by Louis Osman, engraved by Malcolm Appleby with the heraldic symbols and mottos associated with His Royal Highness the Prince of Wales. Above right: this ring in white and yellow gold was designed by Sue Barfield, a British designer who won a Diamonds International Award in 1970. It is decorated with enamel and set with diamonds.*

designers have re-awakened the public to the fascination of original gold work. The artist-jewellers of our time are unquestionably romantics, emotional rather than intellectual, inspired by the minutiae and rhythms of the world around them. They have done things in gold that have never been done before. Though it is not easy to assess contemporary achievements accurately, it seems likely that the work of the second half of this century will be accepted as one of the important periods of goldsmithing, along with the Mycenaean and Etruscan epochs.

But the problem of the artist today is the accelerated pace of change which results from modern communications. Ideas will be seized, diluted into mass-produced commercial pieces, exhausted and forgotten as fashion is forced upon fashion without pause. Already the factories and the larger workshops

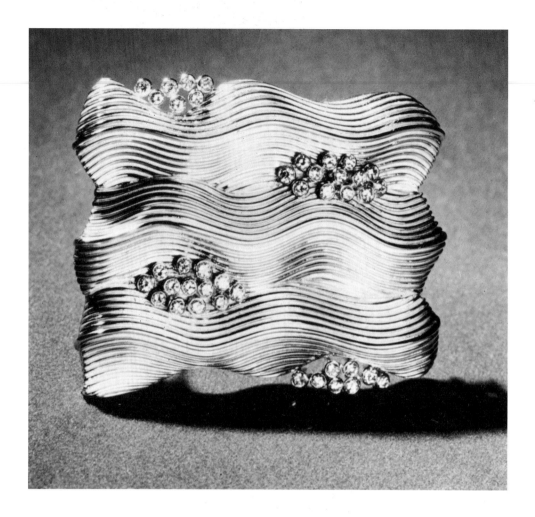

A brooch in white and green gold, set with diamonds, by the Japanese designer Suzuki.

are imitating the new designers' creations with rough-textured wedding rings, nugget-like lighters and the use of natural crystal. Such a general acceptance and repetition of an art form virtually guarantees its decay, and a new movement must arise to demand freedom from its debased conventions.

The goldsmiths of Ancient Egypt made a single style last for more than 2,500 years. Mycenae had one which endured for half a millennium. But in our restless age the possibilities of a style can be burnt out in a decade. And, as we scan the creative horizon wondering what may be coming to replace it, we begin to ask what is the future of the golden arts.

Part Two

8

The Golden Regalia of Europe

The first royal head-dress of which we have any record was the symbol of Uraeus, the cobra god, which the kings of Egypt wore wrought in gold on their brows. The kings of the Persians had golden diadems, and the emperors of Rome laurel wreaths. These were the forerunners of the golden crowns which for a thousand years the Christian church has placed upon the heads of monarchs in Europe, Africa, India, Latin America, and the Pacific islands in affirmation of their divine right to rule. But that right was to be hugely challenged, and few thrones remain in Europe today. Only the United Kingdom retains the traditional coronation ceremony, with the head of the church presiding over the solemn crowning and the taking of the oath.

The Byzantine emperors were the first to incorporate a cross in their crowns, probably as early as the 4th century. The 9th-century Byzantine stemma had two crossbands or arches, usually with a cross at the intersection and long pendants at the sides, decorated with gemstones. These arched crowns seem to have developed from the imperial helmets of earlier rulers, in which the spaces between were filled with leather or metal plates to protect the wearer. They spread into Europe between A.D. 500 and 600. Charles the Bold and Edward the Confessor are both depicted in crowns of this type.

Left: *the ampulla and spoon of the English regalia. They are used in anointing the sovereign with holy oil during the coronation ceremony. British Crown copyright reserved.*

Some European countries adopted a later Byzantine royal head-dress, the conical cap enriched with gold and gems and called *kamelaukion*.

Among the Germanic tribes the king had been traditionally presented with a helmet, a lance and a sword. The helmet became the crown. The sword came to symbolise the king's duty to protect his people and defend the faith. The lance evolved into the sceptre, which often ended in a globe surmounted by a cross, meaning the church's dominion over the world. In 11th-century Germany the crown, sword and sceptre were augmented by an orb and spurs, the latter signifying the king's knightly prowess as a warrior. These five symbols, with the ampulla to hold the anointing oil, were to remain the most important items of royal regalia down the centuries.

Some of the actual coronation crowns were virtually unwearable. The one which the widow of the Saxon king Henry V brought to England in the 12th century was so heavy that 'it is borne to and fro supported by two silver rods. It requires the full strength of a man's two arms when it is taken up to the treasury strong room.' Another monstrous crown, the Corona Oloferni, was seized from the camp of Frederick II in 1248 while he was out hunting. 'It was as great as a cauldron for it was rather for dignity and for great price than for his head . . .' In Plantagenet times it was customary for a king to wear a crown over his helmet in the field. For these and other reasons, monarchs had a multiplicity of crowns if their countries could afford them. Charles V of France and his queen had 41 between them. There were also reliquary crowns to deck the statues of royal and saintly persons, and others of iron and gilt bronze which were more often buried with dead kings than the costly golden originals. Despite wars, revolutions and the disappearance of empires, at least 200 of the crowns of Europe have survived.

The Royal Regalia of England

Of all the surviving regalia the English is the most sumptuous. It is all relatively recent in date, for in 1649 the Commonwealth ordered the earlier crowns, orbs, sceptres and maces to be melted down and turned into coinage. Only the golden ampulla was made before the Restoration. An eagle with spread wings, it is believed to have been made in the 14th century, though chased decoration characteristic of 17th-century work has been added.

The most important of the crowns is St Edward's Crown, traditionally used in the coronation service, but exchanged for the lighter Crown of State during the latter part of the ceremony. Edward the Confessor was the last of the Anglo-Saxon kings, crowned at Winchester in 1043 and canonised in

1161. The St Edward's Crown used before the civil war, whether it was really his or not, was 'totallie broken and defaced' with the rest. Apparently it had a fleur-de-lis motif, a royal device first used by Constantine the Great, above the circlet. It was replaced with the other regalia for the coronation of Charles II by Sir Robert Vyner, his court goldsmith. Legends that the new crown was made from the gold of the original do not seem credible.

The weight of St Edward's Crown is 4 lb 15 oz, and it was a regular practice in the past for borrowed jewels to be set in its frame for coronations and removed afterwards. A coronation inventory of James II includes an item under this crown: 'For the loan of jewels returned . . . £500.' Another £960 was paid for the hire of £24,000 worth of jewels to set in it for the coronation of Queen Anne.

In 1671, shortly after the new regalia had been placed in the Jewel House of the Tower of London, the famous Colonel Blood made his attempt to steal it. He and his three companions tied up Talbot Edwards, the 80-year-old custodian of the treasure, but the old man's son appeared and raised an alarm. The raiders made off with the Crown of State and the orb, but Blood and another of them were captured and the pieces recovered. Charles II was so amused by Blood's audacity that instead of ordering his execution, as was generally expected, he enrolled him in his bodyguard and allowed him a pension of £500 a year.

George IV was not crowned with St Edward's Crown, nor were the next three monarchs. For his coronation in 1821 George IV had a new crown made by Rundell and Bridge, who charged £735 for it plus a hiring fee of £6,525 for the stones. These were not returned, and further charges were made for them. The frame of this crown is now kept in the London Museum. William IV is believed to have been crowned with the old Imperial State Crown of Charles II. Victoria used a golden circlet made for George IV and then a new Imperial Crown, whose stones included the so-called 'Black Prince's ruby' said to have been in the helmet of Henry V at the battle of Agincourt (it is in fact a red spinel of 170 carats). St Edward's Crown was in Westminster Abbey during the coronation of Edward VII, though he did not use it in the ceremony. It came into its own again at the coronation of George V in 1911 and has been used ever since.

A number of other English crowns exist. Among them are a circlet used at the joint coronation of William and Mary in 1689, a little crown made for Queen Victoria, and two pretty ones designed for the 20th-century consorts Mary and Elizabeth. The graceful Imperial Crown of India had to be made specially for George V before he was enthroned at the Delhi Durbar, for the laws of England prevented any of the regalia from being taken out of the country. Louis Osman's modern crown for the investiture of the Prince of Wales was made by the technique of electro-forming, in which gold is electrically deposited on a plastic mould in the plating bath. This process makes it possible to create gold structures thinner and lighter than those usual when traditional methods are employed.

Among the other English regalia there is Vyner's orb which has a circlet and arch heavily set with pearls and gems, with a jewelled cross finial. The smaller and simpler queen's orb was made for Mary II. The royal sceptre, nowadays delivered to the monarch as the ensign of kingly power and justice, was introduced in England by King Edgar in the 10th century. The present sceptre owes its magnificence to the 516.5 carat Star of Africa, cut from the Cullinan diamond and built into it below the cross in the reign of Edward VII. There are two queen's sceptres, one with a cross and one with a dove. The dove appears again on the 'rod of equity and mercy' which is presented to the monarch with an exhortation to guide the people. It is enamelled white, and the rod itself is of gold set with rubies, diamonds and emeralds. The Queen's ivory rod is mounted with gold enriched with enamel, and St Edward's staff, carried by an attendant at coronations, is a 56 inch

Right: *gold coin minted at Oxford for King Charles I during the Civil War and, below, a so-called Calais Noble of Edward III; it shows the king standing on a ship. British Museum. Over page: sixteen gold coins and medals from different periods showing faces and reverses.* Top row, left to right: *gold medal of Napoleon Bonaparte by Denon and Andrieu; curious coin struck in Peru in 1738; 50-franc gold piece struck in Ecuador in 1862; 10-dollar piece, the eagle, struck in the United States in 1799. Second row: 50-dollar octagonal gold piece struck in the U.S.A. in 1851; sovereign of thirty shillings, Elizabeth I of England 1592–5; 4-ducat lamb coin struck in Nuremburg in 1703. Third row: 20,000-reis piece struck in Minas, Brazil, in 1725; 7-ducat of Sigismund III, minted in 1614; Philip V 8-escudo piece of 1738 from Mexico. Fourth row: Roman aureus of Faustina I; aureus of Nerva; aureus of Faustina I; Carthaginian electrum stater with the head of Persephone, made between 241 and 146* B.C. Bottom row: *gold tetradrachm depicting Ptolemy II and Arsinoe II with Ptolemy I and Arsinoe I on the reverse; gold pentadrachm of Ptolemy II bearing the head of Ptolemy I.*

Above: *St Edward's Crown. British Crown copyright reserved.*

Left: *the crown used for the coronation of the Prince of Wales in 1969, made by Louis Osman.*

rod of ornamental gold. The gold spurs in the English regalia are of unknown origin.

Of the four royal swords, only one was made by a goldsmith. It was designed for George IV and cost him £6,000. On its matt gold scabbard the Tudor rose, the thistle and the shamrock are displayed in diamonds, rubies and emeralds. The pommel is richly gem-set with a pattern of oak leaves and acorns, and on the guard are more diamonds and an enormous square-cut emerald. Historically, however, the most interesting of the swords is the Curtana, the sword of mercy. It has no point, and according to legend it was the short sword of Ogier the Dane, who was about to kill Charlemagne's son with it when a heavenly voice bade him be merciful. The Curtana is first mentioned among Queen Eleanor's coronation regalia in 1236.

The gold bracelets include a Charles II pair with a rose, thistle, harp and fleur-de-lis in enamel; and a new pair presented by the governments of the Commonwealth for the coronation of Elizabeth II. The 'ring of kingly dignity' which the sovereign wears on the third finger of the left hand has usually been made especially for each coronation. Vyner produced 'a ring with a ruby' for the Restoration. Those of William IV and Victoria are set with a sapphire in a circle of diamonds, and on both of them a gold cross has been built on top of the sapphire and set with emeralds. The ring of Queen Adelaide has a large ruby surrounded by diamonds, and its gold shank is set all round with rubies like an eternity ring.

The Crown of Charlemagne

The German Imperial Crown, sometimes known as the Crown of Charlemagne, or the Nuremberg Crown, is now in the Hofburg in Vienna. It is believed to have been made at the monastery of Reichenau for the coronation of Otto I in 960. The association with Charlemagne, who died a century and a half earlier, is one of continuity rather than contact. This crown was worn by a number of German kings when they entered Rome for their coronation by the Pope as Holy Roman emperors. In modern times it has had a strange and mobile history: spirited off in a dung cart before the French captured Nuremberg, moved twice again to elude Napoleon's soliders, taken back to Vienna in 1813 and returned to Nuremberg at Hitler's command in 1938. During World War II it was hidden in a salt mine, where the Americans found it and returned it to Vienna.

Byzantine in style, it has eight panels of 21 carat gold, pinned together and supported inside with two iron rings. Above the front panel is a cross contemporary with the crown, but probably added later. In 1024 Conrad II

The Crown of Charlemagne, with an illustrated panel showing King Solomon.
The Hofburg, Vienna.

added an arch of 22 carat gold from front to back. Empty sockets are thought to have held gold fleur-de-lis and gemstone pendants. The crown is heavily loaded both with gems and symbolism, starting with the panels. Eight is a magic number representing infinity and the eternal afterlife. All the stones have magic significance, and the back plate is supposed to be a reproduction of the High Priest's Robe. The champlevé enamelling depicts Old Testament scenes. On the arch the inscription '*Chuonradus dei gratia Romanoru Imperator Aug.*' is carried out in pearls held by gold wires.

With the crown in the Hofburg treasury is a 24 carat gold orb which shared its adventures. Made in the 12th century, it is of six plates soldered together and decorated with bands of filigree. The Byzantine cross is in 21 carat gold and was probably an addition. Both this and one of the arches are set with gemstones.

The Crowns of France

Of all the ancient regalia of France, only three gold crowns are left. The rest was melted down in 1790 after the Revolution, and when three years later Barrière suggested that 'the frightful souvenirs of the former kings' should be destroyed the citizens of Paris broke open 51 royal tombs and despoiled them.

The oldest of the three is a reliquary crown of the 13th century, now in the treasury of Amiens Cathedral. It is a gold circle above which rise six large and six small fleurs-de-lis. It was once heavily set with large stones, but most of the settings are now empty. This crown is typical of those worn by the early French kings when they adopted the lily as their symbol. The other two crowns are in the Louvre. One was made by the king's jeweller, Laurent Ronde, for Louis XV after his coronation in 1722. Above a circlet rise eight fleurs-de-lis from which eight arches develop, and the finial is a three-dimensional fleur-de-lis, the central stone of which was once the pear-shaped Sancy diamond. The Regent diamond of 136.75 carats was set into the fleur-de-lis at the front. The satin bonnet of royal purple within the arches was enriched with 25 more diamonds, and every available space on the gold frame was crammed with important stones. This was one of the most magnificent crowns ever to leave a royal workshop. But today it looks a little tawdry, for the stones have been replaced with paste replicas.

Compared with this spectacular headpiece, the crown made for Napoleon's coronation in 1804 looks utilitarian. He had wanted to have the Crown of Charlemagne for the ceremony, but his troops never located its Austrian hiding place, and this new crown was produced instead. It retains the symbolism of eight, with the arches rising from laurel leaves on the circlet. It is decorated with cameos and has an orb finial surmounted by a cross.

The Bohemian Regalia

The Crown of St Wenceslas.

The finest example of a medieval royal crown is that in the cathedral of St Vitus in Prague. The Crown of St Wenceslas was made for Charles IV in 1347. He had been brought up at the French court, and it consists of four giant gold fleur-de-lis pinned together and set with large stones. Tradition has it that the cross above its two intersecting arches contains a thorn from the Crown of Thorns. The coronations of the queens as well as the kings of Bohemia were solemnised with this crown, and the ceremonies were held on different days. The orb and sceptre are masterpieces of goldsmithing in the Renaissance style. The orb is of 18 carat gold and weighs 780 grammes. It is divided by a horizontal band set with gemstones and pearls, and above and below this are chased repoussé religious scenes. On top of the globe is a cast-chased pedestal depicting sphinxes and acanthus leaves, and from this rises a beautiful gem-set enamelled and cast-chased cross. The sceptre has a cylindrical baluster staff with large bosses foliate chased all over. Those above and below the grip are set with pearls, and the grip itself has a pattern of vine leaves in champlevé enamel. The complicated finial has a design of S-scrolls decorated with chased acanthus work and set with more gems and pearls. Both these splendid pieces were made for the coronation of the art-loving Rudolph II in 1575.

The Austrian Crowns

Up to the reign of Rudolph IV the rulers of Austria had the title of Duke, and from then up to 1804 they were styled Archdukes, and were crowned with an archducal hat made for Maximilian III in 1616 and contained in a gold framework of eight triangular plates tipped with pearls, set with gems and decorated with enamel. Two crossed arches rise to a finial in the form of a small orb bearing a gem-set cross. Maximilian entrusted the hat to the monastery of Klosterneuburg, where it is still preserved, but reserved to himself and his successors the right to remove it for 30 days. When Joseph II wished to enter Frankfurt wearing it for his coronation in 1764 the monks obstinately refused to lend it to him, and he had to have a new one made for the occasion. The newer hat, with 12 triangles and a single arch, is in the Hofburg in Vienna.

Many of the Archdukes were also emperors, and the Hofburg also houses the Imperial Crown, sceptre and orb. The crown was made in the 16th century for Rudolph V, who was a great patron of goldsmithing and attracted many Milanese gem-cutters to the royal workshop he founded in Prague. It is a gem-set gold circlet with rising fleur-de-lis and the single arch associated with imperial crowns. On top is a tiny cross surmounted by a huge egg-shaped sapphire. The unusual feature of this crown is the two gold panels on either side of the arch which give it something of the character of a mitre. These are beautifully repoussé chased, showing Rudolph as a conqueror and in coronation processions. The panels are edged with broad bands enamelled with insects, birds, flowers and fruit and fringed with fine pearls.

The imperial orb has a large gem-set cross, and its circlet is similar to the one on the crown. The enamel decoration on the encircling arches is very similar too. The sceptre has an ivory stem, a richly enamelled grip and a complex head set with gems. These two pieces were added to the imperial regalia by Matthias, who became Archduke of Austria and emperor in 1612.

The Imperial Crown made for Rudolph II when he became Holy Roman Emperor in the 16th century. The Hofburg, Vienna.

The Ancient Crowns of Bavaria

A treasury particularly rich in royal relics is the Schatzkammer der Residenz in Munich. In the medieval room are a crown made at the beginning of the 11th century and another dating from the mid-14th century. The first is a circlet of five rectangular plates set with gems and decorated with filigree, riveted to a gold backing ring. It is similar to the famous Iron Crown of Monza, though simpler. Kunigunde, daughter of Siegfried, Count of Luxemburg, may have worn it when she married Henry the Saint, Duke of Bavaria, and was crowned in 1002. The other crown is of silver gilt, French in style, with fleur-de-lis on a circlet with a stylised cross in front. At one time these two crowns were joined together and placed on the skull of the Empress of Bavaria, patron saint of Bamberg, at festivals.

The Schatzkammer also contains the lovely 14th-century crown thought to have been made for Princess Blanche, daughter of Henry IV of England. She married the Elector Louis III of the Palatinate in 1402.

The Russian Regalia

The early years of the Russian monarchy were even more strife-torn than those at its end. Between the 11th and 13th centuries there were 83 civil wars, with 290 princes claiming the succession of the 64 principalities. Amid all this upheaval, the Tartar hordes of Genghis Khan swept across the country in 1224. It was not until the 15th century that a more or less stable empire was created by Ivan III and coronations took place.

After the Turks captured Constantinople in 1453 Russia became the stronghold of the Eastern church, and her crown was of the Byzantine hat type, Russianised by the addition of a wide circlet of fur. The earliest surviving crown from the Tsars' coronations is thought to be that of Vladimir II Monomachus, who ruled from 1113 to 1125. Its eight filigree panels have large stones in box settings, and pearls riveted through. Over its dome is a pearl-decorated cross.

A number of other crowns of similar form are in the Kremlin Museum. The Crown of Astrakhan, a richly set and enamelled gold cap, was used for the coronation of Tsar Michael Theodorovitch. The so-called Crown of Kazan is made of *opus interrasile* panels, a favourite Byzantine style of decoration. Then there are the two diamond-encrusted caps which belonged to the brothers Ivan V and Peter I, who were crowned together in 1682. Catherine I, who succeeded her husband Peter the Great in 1724, was crowned with a mitre similar in design to the Imperial Crown in Vienna, and its framework is in the Kremlin. So is a pretty mitre crown made for the Empress Anna Ivanova.

The Russian Imperial Crown, made for the coronation of Catherine II in 1762, resembles the fashionable jewellery of that period in that the gold frame is concealed almost completely behind a composition of stones. It is set with 2,075 diamonds weighing nearly 1,400 carats. Among the rest of

The Crown of Astrakhan. The Kremlin, Moscow.

the flamboyant regalia which the Russian people queue to see is one piece of outstanding beauty, the orb of Tsar Michael. It is Renaissance work, 16th century or earlier. The globe is decorated with champlevé enamel scenes from the life of David. Diamonds, emeralds and sapphires in heavy and prominent box settings decorate the circlet, the arch and the great foot-high cross. The peculiar footed orb which Ivan Jouriev supplied to Tsar Alexis Michael in 1662 at a cost of 7,917 roubles is by comparison a heavy and uninspired piece of royal goldsmithing.

Ancient Italian Crowns

Two of Italy's historic Lombardic crowns lie today in Monza cathedral, which stands on the site of a 6th-century church founded by Queen Theolinda. Her simple golden circlet is set now with mother-of-pearl instead of its original half-pearls, and many of its missing gems have been replaced by paste replicas. Her husband's Crown of Agilulf no longer exists. It was

The Iron Crown of Lombardy. Monza Cathedral, Italy.

stolen and partly melted down in 1804 in Paris, where Napoleon had taken the Monza treasures on proclaiming himself king of Italy.

The second Monza survivor, known as the Iron Crown, has six gold plates with floral motifs in cloisonné enamel, and is enriched with cabochon gemstones. The plates are attached to an iron ring traditionally supposed to have been forged from a nail of the True Cross. Though there is little historical evidence for this, the cathedral continues to treat this crown as a holy relic. It is believed to date from the 9th century and from the 11th was regularly used for coronations, including the Napoleonic ceremony.

In Palermo Cathedral is a Byzantine-style cap with gem-set gold ornaments attached. It may have belonged to the emperor Frederick II, for it was found in the grave of his wife Constance of Aragon, who died in 1222 while still in her twenties. This piece, which is probably of Sicilian workmanship, is thought to have been placed in the tomb to express the emperor's grief.

St Stephen's Crown

The Crown of St Stephen, the famous coronation treasure of Hungary, has seldom been made available for inspection, and most of our information about it comes from a monograph by P. J. Kelleher published in 1951. The US Army gave him access to the crown when it was in their hands at the end of the war.

It is a broad circlet to which enamel plaques depicting saints have been attached in the Byzantine manner. Huge cabochon gems are set into it. Integral with the circlet are two semi-circular shields. The front one shows in champlevé enamel the Pantocrator seated on a throne between two trees. The one at the back has an enamelled portrait of the 11th-century Byzantine emperor Michael Dukas, and on the circlet to its left is a similar portrait of the Hungarian king Geza. Flanking the front shield are triangular and semi-circular motifs decorated with abstract patterns in cloisonné enamel edged with filigree and surmounted by diamond beads riveted through. Rising above the crown, two arches bear further enamelled panels, one showing Christ.

The most widely recognised feature of St Stephen's Crown is its finial – a lopsided cross with ball terminals. Some experts believe it was designed to lean in this way, but others think it was damaged at some time.

Kelleher said that this noble relic was a copy of a Byzantine emperor's crown, as worn by two of them in the miniature of the Vatican Psalter. 'There can be no doubt', he wrote, 'that the arch and the gabled enamels are of

Left: the Crown of St Stephen. This object has mysteriously disappeared.

Byzantine origin.' He believed that the various elements in it were put together to provide a dynastic crown for Hungary between 1108 and 1116.

Ancient Crowns of Spain

Considering the stiff etiquette that always prevailed at the Spanish court, it surprises many to learn that the country abandoned formal coronations in the 14th and 15th centuries and that it has no true royal regalia of its own. There are, however, six Visigothic crowns in the National Archaeological Museum in Madrid. Some are too small to be worn and were obviously made as reliquary crowns. Two large ones at least could have been royal crowns, possibly all that is left of the 25 crowns or diadems 'adorned with precious stones, belonging to the monarchs who ruled the land' which the Moors found when they entered the church at Tarik in the 8th century.

The surviving crowns are simple gem-set gold circlets similar to the Monza examples, but with pendant fringes. The fringes on the two large ones spell out the names of the kings Recevinthus and Svinthila in letters cut from gold sheet. Chains have been added to suspend the crowns, and on the big pair these consist of heart-shaped links. All these Visigothic crowns are thought to have been hidden at some time, and peasants sold them to jewellers in Toledo in 1858. They were later smuggled to France and were in the Cluny Museum in Paris until 1940, when they were returned to Spain on loan.

The Swedish Regalia

When Charles VIII visited the monastery at Vadstena in 1455:

> A crown of gold on his head he wore,
> A golden orb in his right hand he bore,
> And in his left hand a golden sceptre.
> And a knight went before him with a naked gilded sword.

All this has disappeared, with the rest of Sweden's ancient regalia, including the crown the 'goldsmiths' swains' of Stockholm made for Gustavus I in 1528. The earliest surviving items of the present regalia are the crown and sceptre made in 1561 for the coronation of Eric XIV. These two pieces are by Cornelius ver Weiden, a Flemish goldsmith working in Stockholm, and the accompanying orb may be by his brother Peter.

The crown is very ornate, an enamelled gold circlet encrusted with gemstones and pearls. Large foliate ornaments, similarly encrusted, soar up from the circlet. The crossed arches dip, supporting an orb which is enamelled blue and scattered with golden stars, and on top stands a large diamond-set cross. The sceptre originally had a globe cut from a single large sapphire, but this has been replaced by an intricate enamelled head. The Swedish 'Orb of the Realm' has a map of the world chased on its sphere, and thus is unique among crown jewels. The king of Sweden is no longer crowned, but the regalia is used when he opens parliament, at which time it stands on a table beside the throne. Otherwise it is kept in the strong room of the State Bank, together with the gold ampulla made for Charles IX in 1606. This is a Renaissance horn with a foot and baluster stem. The mouth of the horn is lidded and at the other end is a figure holding a pair of scales. The vessel is decorated with translucent white and coloured enamels.

Another ancient crown preserved in Sweden is the Goslar reliquary, believed to have been looted from a German cathedral. It is a circlet attached to a gold-mounted agate bowl which is reputed to hold the skull of a saint.

———

Other existing crowns of Europe include the charming little Scottish one which was made in 1539 and is in Edinburgh Castle; the papal triple crowns in the Vatican treasury; and the crowns of Denmark, Holland, Norway and Portugal, all made in the 19th century. The making of crowns occupied the skills of many of the leading Continental goldsmiths during a period of over 1,500 years. But most of the kingdoms have vanished with their regalia and the monarchs who wore it. That so much should have been guarded and preserved nevertheless demonstrates the powerful symbolic force of these golden tokens, a force equally implicit in the determination of the French revolutionaries to destroy them.

9
Gold Coins

Gold had a long history as a medium of exchange before the first coins were struck from it. In Egypt the Pharaohs had used it to buy not only goods, but political support as well. The standard-weight gold rings produced there and elsewhere were obviously a form of money, and the coming of coinage might have seemed at the start to be merely a formalisation of a system already in existence. Its effects, however, were to be much more far-reaching both on individuals and on society as a whole. It meant, among other things, that transactions in gold were no longer limited to dealings between one king and another, for now merchants could conduct them too. A range of specialised crafts and professions emerged, all concerned with the manufacture and manipulation of money, including coiners, mint-masters and money-changers. As the money-changers acquired more respect and influence, they became bankers. Monarchs began to see their gold coinage as a potent symbol of their prestige, as important as their golden regalia, and this too was to have far-reaching consequences.

It was the kings of Lydia who were responsible for giving gold this new economic significance. The Lydians were successful merchants and expert craftsmen, and their administrative classes had a high standard of living. Herodotus described them as 'the first men to have struck and used gold and silver coins'. These were little lentil-shaped blobs of electrum, bearing a series of crude punch marks and almost certainly issued on the orders of King Ardys in about 640 B.C. The punching on later Lydian coins was more sophisticated, showing heraldic animals. The most famous were the devices of King Croesus, the head of a lion and the facing heads of a lion and a bull. He had these struck about 560 B.C. on what is accepted as the first gold coinage in the world, the beautiful Lydian gold staters.

The Persians who overran Lydia soon adopted gold and silver coinage. The soldiers of King Darius and the craftsmen who built Persepolis were paid in coins bearing a full-length figure in Persian costume, presumably intended to represent Darius himself. It was the Greeks, however, who developed early money into the kind of coin we know, a flat disc with relief designs on each side. Owls, bees, ears of wheat and goddesses appeared on the silver coins of Athens, Corinth, Rhodes and other city-states. Only later, with the Thracian mines in production and wealth flowing in from the conquests of

Alexander the Great, did Greece turn to a gold coinage. The Macedonian gold stater, the first Greek gold coin, was tiny, with the profile of Apollo on one side and a chariot on the reverse.

The Ptolemies, the last royal house of Egypt before the Romans came, were the first rulers to have their profiles cut into dies and impressed on gold coins, starting about 305 B.C. A gold tetradrachm, sold at Christies in 1970, is a dynastic picture gallery in miniature. On one side Ptolemy I and his queen are shown, and on the other are profiles of Ptolemy II and his sister-wife, Arsinoe II.

The early Romans, as we have seen, were even worse off for precious metals than the Greeks, and it was only in the first century B.C. that a gold coinage was introduced. Previous Roman coins, struck from copper and then silver, bore portraits of the gods and the dead. Julius was the first Caesar to put his own head on a piece of money – and within two years of the issue of these gold portrait coins he was murdered.

The Romans made various attempts to discourage the practice of clipping and filing, by which unscrupulous citizens were able to remove precious metal from coins. Among these safeguards were serrated edges and circular beaded designs. The former was discontinued in later Roman coins (though Charles II, after a good deal of effort, made the English mint accept milled edges in 1663, and they have since become a feature of higher-value coins). Such precautions cannot have been very effective in Rome, because there were other ways to get metal off, such as washing and sweating; and in any case the design of the coin itself was seldom truly struck or the blank symmetrical.

A frieze on a house in Pompeii shows stages of coin production at this time, with winged cherubs representing the slaves who actually carried out the work. First the metal is melted in a furnace, which is blown with bellows. The metal is poured and shaped and the blank weighed. A cherub with pincers holds the lower die on an anvil and the blank is laid on top. The other cherub strikes it with the upper die held in a haft, and the face and obverse designs are impressed simultaneously.

When Rome fell to the Barbarians and the centre of Roman power shifted to Constantinople, the Byzantine empire became a great gold power. Its gold coinage was of high quality, but artistically a little disappointing. The typical gold solidus showed the emperor's bust in a meagre relief pattern of lines and dots. In solidi of the 7th and 8th centuries the images of Heraclius and Justinian II are accompanied by those of their sons. The Byzantine cross is usually incorporated, and sometimes Christ or the Virgin. On some coins the cross appears on its own; and during the iconoclastic period, when religious images were prohibited, calligraphy replaced the representational designs.

The Germanic kings of Europe continued to operate the Roman mints or started new ones. Some, like the Frankish king Theodebart, had a confusing habit of issuing copies of Byzantine solidi bearing his name and the emperor's portrait. Strangely, all the new coins issued on the Continent for several centuries after the fall of Rome seem to have been of gold, although large-scale gold mining had come to a halt. During this period the Burgundians in France and the Anglo-Saxons in England were putting out gold money; and up to the Moorish conquest in 711 the Visigothic kings in Spain issued a succession of little gold triens from their well organised mints. The extent of minting at this time is illustrated by the treasure from the Sutton Hoo ship burial: each of the 38 gold coins in it came from a different French mint.

A period followed during which the silver penny and the silver denier were the standard coins of Europe, and it was not until the 13th century that gold coins were again struck. The first of these was the Brindisi Augustale, a coin of classical style which made a brief appearance under Frederick II. Next came the famous Venetian gold ducat, and then the gold florin, issued by Florence and taking its name from it.

Philip IV of France, known as *le roi faux monnayeur*, is chiefly remembered for debasing his country's coinage (one of many expedients was the introduction of a sales tax, to which he was driven in financing his war against England). Yet it was he who gave Europe its first gold coin in the Gothic style, the beautiful masse d'or. It depicted the crowned king sitting on his throne, sceptre in hand. Louis IX issued the smaller heraldic écu d'or, which had a shield bearing the royal fleur-de-lis in a Gothic frame.

The écu and the Italian florin dominated European currency throughout the 14th century, but Edward III tried to challenge their ascendancy by issuing an English gold florin in 1344. It showed him enthroned against a ground of the fleur-de-lis. This coin had a short life and was replaced in the 1360s by the larger gold noble which depicted Edward standing in a ship with his shield on his arm, possibly in commemoration of his naval victory at the battle of Sluys. England's population had been reduced by more than one-third by the Black Death; she and the French were locked in the Hundred Years' War; a major social and economic crisis was spreading; a peasants' revolt was brewing; and the goldsmiths and merchants of the City of London were organising a public inquiry into the state of English currency. But despite all these tribulations, these medieval gold coins, particularly the French ones, are perhaps the most beautiful coins ever minted, with the possible exception of the silver coinage of Greece. They have a freedom and freshness seldom seen since.

The great fairs of the Middle Ages drew merchants from many different countries. Among them the money-changers set up their tables. They also lent money to the merchants, and from such small beginnings great banking businesses grew. But while the word of a trader might be reliable, the money quite often was not. Even threats of the death penalty did not scare off the clippers and counterfeiters, and Edward III eventually established the 'trial of the pyx'. Coins are chosen at random and placed in a wooden box, or pyx, and assayed for purity. This ritual is still held every year at Goldsmiths' Hall in London. On the Continent rulers were apparently making similarly strenuous efforts to standardise the coinage, but in fact it had been discovered, especially in France, that calling in existing coinage and replacing it with debased money was a convenient method of taxing the merchant class. Under the modern name of currency reform, this tactic has been used by totalitarian states or dictatorships to wipe out the profits of unauthorised speculators.

The mechanised production of money was brought nearer by an invention of Leonardo da Vinci. 'No coin can be considered good which does not have the rim perfect', he wrote; and in the critical world of the Renaissance this statement was readily accepted. He designed a punching machine to produce coin blanks. Drawings of it in his notebooks have beside them his satisfied observation: 'This cuts coins of perfect roundness, thickness and weight, and saves the need of the man who cuts and weighs and saves also the man who makes coins round. They pass therefore merely through the hands of the worker of the plate and the stamper and they are fine coins.'

The screw press, which replaced the striking of coins on an anvil, was another 16th-century invention, usually attributed to the Italian medallist Donato Bramante. It was opposed by the moneyers, as craftsmen have opposed so many technical innovations. Henry II of France put a press into the Moulin des Etuves in 1551, and it produced excellent coins, including the double Henri d'or bearing the seated figure of Gallia on the reverse. But agitation by the other French moneyers led to coining there being discontinued 11 years later. In England, when a Huguenot named Eloi Mestrel set up a press in the Tower of London in 1561 the Warden of the Mint closed it down, and the unlucky pioneer was later hanged for 'coining' or counterfeiting. In 1640 Louis XIII mechanised a French mint at the Louvre, which struck the fine pieces of eight and 10 louis d'or. These were engraved by the mint-master, Jean Varin, with splendid high relief profiles of the king.

The great Italian families had similar coins with their high relief portraits struck in the cities they ruled: the Sforzas in Milan, Giovanni il Bentivoglio in Bologna, and Francesco il Gonzaga in Mantua. The last two are among the most unflattering heads ever put on coins. Giovanni is every inch the pugnacious *condottiere*, and Francesco epitomises the weak and wavering monarch. Florence and Venice were loath to follow the trend, for their florins and ducats were too well established as international trading coins for their look to be tampered with, and besides the Medicis were at pains to appear democratic. Not until the 16th century did a Medici portrait appear on coins. Although the new mint-master responsible for them was none other than Cellini, these first Florentine portrait coins were very dull indeed.

At the end of the 15th century, under Henry VII, England issued the £1 gold piece called the 'souveraigne' which was to become the eventual symbol of British prosperity. It was not greatly different in style from the Edward III florin, but the reverse side has a Renaissance opulence, with the royal arms in the centre of the stylised Tudor rose. The sovereign, however, by no means reached its stable supremacy overnight, owing to the sharp monetary practice of the next king, Henry VIII. It is interesting to compare the amount of personal gold he is wearing in that overloaded Holbein painting with the debasement and degeneration he caused in the English currency after his father's death. He levied a forced loan on the kingdom, though it brought in very little; he forced the mints to reduce the fineness of gold to 23 carats; he watered down silver money from full-standard sterling to a dismaying alloy which contained only 4 oz of silver to 12 oz of copper per pound; he produced inflation, financial panic and rebellion. When his daughter Elizabeth became queen she put a stop to the bad money and restored the standards from which Britain's financial prestige could grow.

With such cynical policies followed before long by the increasing use of machinery, it is perhaps not surprising that coins gradually lost much of their beauty and artistic appeal. The fly-press was replaced by the mechanical press, and dies were engraved by the new pantographic equipment. The 18th-century louis d'or were a far cry from those of 100 years earlier. And after the general decimalisation of continental coinage the French large denominations of the 19th century look exactly what they are – mass-produced utilitarian pieces of money. The curious English guinea, struck from Guinea gold and worth 21 silver shillings, showed the same degeneration. A Charles II five-guinea piece bears the king's likeness struck from dies sunk by a master engraver, but the portrait on a mid-18th-century guinea has become formal and lifeless. And vigour and individuality were further sapped as coin designs came to be selected by committees.

America at first had no coinage of her own, and all manner of foreign coins were brought over by settlers, and guineas, écus, and Spanish doubloons circulated there freely. Merchants carried scales and gave change on the basis of a coin's intrinsic value. Some copper coins were struck in America in the 17th and 18th centuries, but it was not until after the War of Independence that a regular mint was set up. A gold coinage was authorised in 1792, and three years later the first half-eagles were issued. Valued at $5, they had the head of Liberty on one side and an eagle on the reverse. Gold eagles and quarter-eagles were struck shortly afterwards, and from 1836 they came in increasing volume from the steam presses of the United States mint. An unusual $50 gold piece was issued in 1851. A rare departure from the disc format, it was octagonal and had an eagle on one side and a target on the reverse. (Other variations from the round include the shield-shaped Japanese obans and kobans minted at the same period, and the square four-ducat lambs made in Nuremberg in 1703.) The American $20 gold piece was minted in the late 19th century and at the beginning of the 20th.

Latin American countries have issued many interesting gold coins, though most of their 18th and 19th century ones carry portraits in the classical revivalist style. A strange Peruvian eight-escudo piece struck in Lima in 1738 looks like a medieval coin designed under Byzantine influence. Nineteenth-century Bolivian coins of the same value had the sun, a mountain and a llama on the the obverse. A Brazilian 20,000 reis of John V, struck at Minas Geraes in 1725, is unconventional in having an heraldic design on the face, like the earlier French coinage. The 19th-century gold coins of Ecuador resemble contemporary European coins; they have the profile of the reigning head of state on the face and an heraldic motif on the obverse. Sometimes, however, as on a piece of 1862, this Ecuadorean heraldry is in a distinctly Latin American baroque style.

The 20th century has seen the end of the gold coin as currency. Sovereigns, ducats and golden francs are no more than memories now, collector's items in an age of cupro-nickel coins dominated by the paper money first suggested 250 years ago by Benjamin Franklin.

For a time, currency was, in theory at least, freely redeemable in gold. In 1821, Britain established a gold standard, which meant that the coinage was defined in terms of a fixed quantity of gold at a fixed price. For a period of a little over 20 years, between the 1890s and 1914, all the major countries of the world adopted a gold standard. Then World War I brought disruption because the price of gold became subject to the tug of supply and demand.

After the war, some countries, including Britain, returned to the gold standard, but during the crisis years of the early 'thirties, one country after another went off it again, and gold was allowed to find its own price level. In the last 30 years, the price of gold has risen more rapidly than it did in the previous six centuries. In 1334, in Britain, an ounce of gold was valued at just over 22 shillings. By the 16th century, it had risen to 45 shillings, and by the 17th century to 86 shillings. Then the price was stabilised at 84 shillings an ounce, but between the 'thirties and 1969, gold rose to the record figure of 340 shillings an ounce in Britain.

The US dollar since 1933 has been fixed in terms of gold, at the rate of $35 an ounce. After several scares and revaluations in the 1960s, the international gold market is now divided into two separate sectors. In the so-called official sector, gold is bought and sold among the state banks of the nations at the fixed dollar rate. There is also, however, a 'free' market in which gold finds its own price level according to supply and demand, so that collectors, jewellers, and goldsmiths are still able to operate.

The Refining of Gold and its Hallmarks

The refining of gold probably dates from before 3000 B.C. The ancient Egyptians removed base metal impurities first, presumably by smelting. Not until about 2000 B.C. did they succeed in removing the other major impurity – silver. From then on they began to refine gold to a purity of about 95 per cent. The original purpose was to improve its working qualities. Later, after King Menes established an official value at the beginning of the 4th century, refining to achieve a standard quality became necessary.

Farther on in history refined gold became the basis for the alloys we call carat golds. Starting nowadays with gold which is four nines (99.99) pure, various qualities of gold are produced, of different degrees of purity and therefore different values. Alloying also gives metals of various colours and working characteristics. An alloy which contains more silver than copper yields a more malleable gold. One with a high copper content gives a redder gold. Cadmium and silver used in an alloy produce a green gold. Iron is added for blue gold, and nickel or palladium for white. The purity of these alloys is expressed in carats. Pure gold is 24 carat, so nine carat contains nine parts of gold to 15 parts of other metals.

———

The first marking of gold to denote its quality was the application of the device of King Menes to 14-gramme bars in the first dynasty of Ancient Egypt. Some provincial Roman bars in the British Museum are stamped with the marks of a pro-consul and a mint-master. The systematic marking of gold wares did not begin, however, until 1300 when England introduced a law to protect the public against the fraudulent use of adulterated gold and silver by dishonest smiths.

The British System

At first only one mark, a leopard's head, was punched into silver and gold. Later other marks were added, indicating the quality, place and date of marking and the maker. Originally all wares were marked in London, but afterwards alloying and marking was made lawful in Chester, Exeter, Glasgow, Newcastle-on-Tyne, Norwich, York and a number of goldsmiths' guilds in smaller centres such as Taunton and Greenock marked their wares. Today Britain has only four assay offices: London, Birmingham, Sheffield and Edinburgh. Their marks for gold wares are as follows:

Quality marks Four qualities are legal in Britain: 9, 14, 18 and 22 carat. The two highest have a crown side by side with the carat number, but Edinburgh uses a thistle instead of the crown. The lower qualities are stamped with the carat number and, beside it, the quantity of pure gold in the alloy expressed as parts per thousand.

Town marks The London mark is the leopard's head, which was shown crowned until 1821. Birmingham's is an anchor. Sheffield uses a York rose on gold wares and a crown on silver. The Edinburgh mark is a three-towered castle.

Chester (closed 1962) used its city arms, three wheatsheaves on a shield. Glasgow (closed 1964) did likewise, its arms consisting of a tree, a bell, a fish and a ring.

Maker's marks Early marks usually repeated devices from the trade signs which hung over smiths' doors. Typical of the 15th century were a jug, a fish, or a bow and arrow. Since 1720 the gold-worker's initials have been used. This mark is registered at the assay office and struck into the piece by the maker before it is submitted for assaying.

The date letter From 1478 British gold and silver wares have carried a letter of the alphabet to denote the year of marking. Cycles of different alphabets have been used down the centuries. Various offices have used several alphabets, begun the cycles at different times and omitted letters. 'I' and 'J' were commonly omitted to avoid confusion. Dating is usually done by referring to the pocket guide by Frederick Bradbury, *British and Irish Silver Assay Office Marks* (J. W. Horthend, Sheffield).

Imports   Gold wares imported to Britain must be submitted for assaying and marking. They are then given a special mark, in a square with cut corners. London's sign is the constellation of Leo. Birmingham's is an equilateral triangle. Sheffield uses the Libra sign and Edinburgh a St Andrew's cross.

OTHER SYSTEMS

Twenty-nine other countries today use forms of hallmarking on gold wares. The following is a brief summary of their systems:

Algeria   Standards: three. Mark: a bunch of grapes in a circle.

Argentina   Standards: two. Marks: the figures 750 and 500 in a rectangle. This system dates from 1959.

Australia   Standards: 9, 12, 14, 18 and 22 carat are legal. Mark: a kookaburra. This system dates from 1923.

Austria   Standards: 986/1000, 900/1000, 750/1000 and 585/1000. Marks: an elephant's head for the three higher qualities, enclosed in a shield with the figures (1), (2) or (3) and the marking office initial – G for Graz, I for Innsbruck, L for Linz and W for Wien (Vienna). A horse's head for the lowest quality. Imports: a bunch of grapes and a vine leaf in differently shaped shields which also include the quality number and office initial.

Gold wares have been tested and hallmarked in Austria since the 14th century, originally by the goldsmiths' guilds. The government-controlled offices date from 1784.

Belgium   Standard: 12 carat only. Mark: a circle followed by quality figure in thousandths (500/1000).

Hallmarking is compulsory and dates from Belgian independence in 1830. Manufacturers usually stamp their own wares, though they may request the Bureau de la Garantie to do it for them.

Bulgaria   Standards: 920/1000, 840/1000, 750/1000, 583/1000, 500/1000 and 330/1000. Mark: a Byzantine-style crown with the letter of the marking office followed by quality figure from 1 to 6. This system dates from 1810.

Canada   Standards: 9, 12, 14 and 18 carat. Mark: a crown in a capital C. Hallmarking is done under a law of 1934.

Czechoslovakia   Standards: 9, 14, 18 and a quality between 21.6 and 23.7 carats. Marks: for the two higher qualities, eagle's head in differently shaped shields with the figures 1 or 2. For 14 carat, a cock's head in a shield with figure 3. For 9 carat, a plover's head with figure 4. The assay office initial appears in a square or circle (Bratislava, Brno, Jabionec, Ostrava or Prague). Imports: in a shield with cut corners, a harp with crowned C above.

Hallmarking in Bohemia began in 1366. Previously unmarked ancient wares are stamped with a thistle in a shield. Between 1939 and 1945 wares were marked separately in Slovakia with the head of a man in traditional Slovak head-dress and the figures 1, 2, 3 or 4. In Czek and Moravia the mark was a rampant lion overstamped with the appropriate figure.

Denmark   Standards: all above 14 carat are legal. Marks: figures showing quality in thousandths, e.g. 585/1000, are applied by the maker: in addition, the assay office will apply the traditional Danish mark of three towers to wares at customer's request, after the piece has been tested. This mark includes the last two figures of the year of marking.

Hallmarking has been carried out in Denmark since the beginning of the 17th century, but standards for precious metals have been legally enforced only since 1961. Government testing is by random sampling. If the tower mark is applied, it guarantees the quality indicated by the maker's mark.

Egypt   Standards: 12, 14, 15, 18, 21 and 23 carat. Mark: the government mark is a flamingo in a square. Quality is indicated by Arabic characters in a square.

Finland   Standards: 969/1000, 750/1000 and 585/1000. Marks: the assay mark is a crown on a background of waves, enclosed in a heart. Quality is marked in figures, date by a letter followed by a number, origin by a device varying from city to city (Helsinki by a boat). The maker has his own mark, making five marks in all. On gold, all but the assay mark are in ovals; on silver, in squares. Imports: a lily in an oval.

Hallmarking is under government control. It is carried out at the assay office of the Ministry of Commerce and Industry in Helsinki, or at one of 30 other centres under the supervision of a magistrate or police officials.

France   Standards: 18, 20 and 22 carat. Marks: an eagle's head only, if tested by touchstone. An eagle's head and figure 1, 2 or 3 in a shield whose shape varies according to the quality, if tested by cupellation. Paris city mark: a royal crown with maker's initial below (since the second half of the fifteenth century). Imports: an owl or a weevil.

There are also special marks: an Egyptian head for export watch cases of lower than 18 carat. A rhinoceros' head for chains or bracelets of a certain size. A dog's head for platinum (bimetallic wares bear marks for both metals).

Gold wares have been assayed and hallmarked under government control since 1797, but the Paris mark dates from the 15th century. Other cities also placed their marks on pieces, and one centre may have had many different marks over a period.

Hungary   Standards: 22, 18, and 14 carat. Marks: for 22 carat – a man's head and the number 22; for 18 – also a man's head, but in a different style, and the number 18; for 14 – a horse's head and the number 14. Imports – a sun, letter K, and the quality-figure in a lozenge.

Ireland   Standards: 9, 14, 18, 20 and 22 carat. Marks: the two lowest qualities have a carat mark stamped at right-angles to the quality figure in thousandths. For 18 a unicorn's head, for 20 a fleur-de-lis, for 22 a crowned harp. Also maker's mark and date letter.

The crowned harp was originally the mark of the Dublin assay office, established by Charles I in 1637. In 1729 a seated figure of Hibernia was added to show that duty on silver had been paid. Since 1807 this has been the Dublin town mark. Cork and other centres had their own marks, stamped by the guilds, at various times.

Israel   Standards: 9, 14, 18 and 21 carat. Marks: a lyre which varies in design and incorporates a quality figure in thousandths. Date letter. Tower mark containing Hebraic characters for the four cities where gold is marked – Haifa, Jerusalem, Nazareth and Tel Aviv. There are special marks for wedding rings and imports.

Compulsory hallmarking of gold dates from 1963. Assaying and marking is by the Israel Standards Institution.

Italy   Standards: 750/1000, 585/1000, 500/1000 and 333/1000. Marks: an ear of corn in a square with figures 1, 2, 3 or 4.

Italy began hallmarking gold early in the 17th century, using a crossed key mark.

Japan   Nine different standards are legal, ranging from 1000/1000 down to 375/1000. Marks: quality figure in a diamond shape next to a flag with a circle on it.

Malta   Standards: 9, 12, 15, 18 and 22 carat. Marks: for the two highest qualities, a castle. For the others, a shield.

Hallmarking was instituted by the Knights of St John of Jerusalem in 1530. Since 1968 it is illegal to sell gold wares unless they have a government mark.

Netherlands   Standards: up to 1853 legal qualities were 916/1000, 853/1000 and 750/1000. Marks: for the two highest qualities, a lion rampant with figure 1 or 2. For lowest, a lion passant. From 1853 to 1953 there was also a permissible quality of 583/1000 which carried a leaf mark. Modern standards since then are: 833/1000 (lion rampant), 750/1000 (lion passant) and 585/1000 (leaf). Quality figures in thousandths appear in the enclosing lozenge. Imports: formerly a G in a lozenge with one, two or no dots. Now a decorative lozenge with quality in thousandths.

Dutch towns used hallmarks from the 14th century and letter dating from the 16th. Marking was centralised between 1800 and 1810. Since 1814 a lion's head mark has also been stamped on gold wares, differing slightly on large and small pieces. A special small goods mark used since 1953.

Norway   Standards: 14 and 18 carat. Marks: a lion rampant with the legend 14K and 18K.

Gold has been hallmarked since the 16th century.

Poland   Standards: 960/1000, 750/1000, 583/1000, 500/1000 and 375/1000. Marks: a helmeted head in a shield with figures 1, 2, 3, 4 or 5.

Portugal   Standards: 800/1000 is the minimum legal standard for gold wares generally. Watches and certain other objects may be made to 750/1000 or 583/1000. Marks: the higher quality has a dog's head with fangs bared and figure 800 below. The lower qualities have the dog's head and figures 1 or 2. Export: a tower with the quality figure above.

Since 1938 Lisbon, Oporto and Gondomar have used slightly differing local marks. Ancient wares bear an old man's head. There are also special marks for bimetallic objects and for certain other categories containing gold.

Gold has been locally hallmarked since the 17th century.

Romania   Standards: Nine qualities ranging from 958/1000 down to 375/1000. Mark: worker in a cap with a hammer on his shoulder.

Hallmarking dates from 1906.

Soviet Union   Standards: 958/1000, 750/1000 and 583/1000. Marks: a man's head and the quality number. These are stamped by the factories and checked by government inspectors.

Hallmarking began in Russia in the 17th century.

Sweden   Standards: 875/1000, 840/1000 and 760/1000. Marks: 23K, 20K or 18K. Since 1901, three crowns on a background of waves in a club-shaped shield. Imports: the same in an oval shield. Date letters have been used in Stockholm since 1968 and in other centres since 1759. Town marks have the initial letter of the name, but Stockholm has a crowned head.

Hallmarking was begun in the 16th century by the town guilds.

Switzerland   Standards: 18 and 14 carat. Marks: the head of Helvetia for 18 and a crouching squirrel for 14. These date from 1882 and have been slightly altered since then. Export wares of higher than the Swiss standard are marked with a Bernese damsel. Export watch cases of lower than the national standard bear a morning star mark. Imported watch cases are marked with the head of a lynx and the figure 1 or 2, for 18 or 14 carat.

Hallmarking was introduced in the cantons of Geneva and Neuchâtel in the 15th century and is now carried out, along with assaying, by the central customs administration in Berne.

Tunisia   Standards: 875/1000, 840/1000, 750/1000 and 583/1000. Marks: for large wares, a horse's head in a shield with quality numbers. Shield and figure vary according to standard. For smaller wares, slightly different horse's head.

The present marks date from 1942. Gold has been hallmarked in Tunisia since 1856.

Turkey   Standards: six qualities from 22 down to 12 carat. Marks: a crescent enclosing the quality figure.

Yugoslavia   Standards: 950/1000, 840/1000, 750/1000 and 583/1000. Marks: for larger wares, the profile of a helmeted, bearded man in a notched shield. For small objects, an ear of corn. Quality numbers from 1 to 4. Imports: a hawk, an eagle's head or a dagger, according to quality. Exports: three leaves in a circle. Bimetallic wares have special marks, a stoat for those of gold and silver and a dolphin for gold and platinum.

Below are illustrated some of the most interesting marks discussed in the previous chapter.

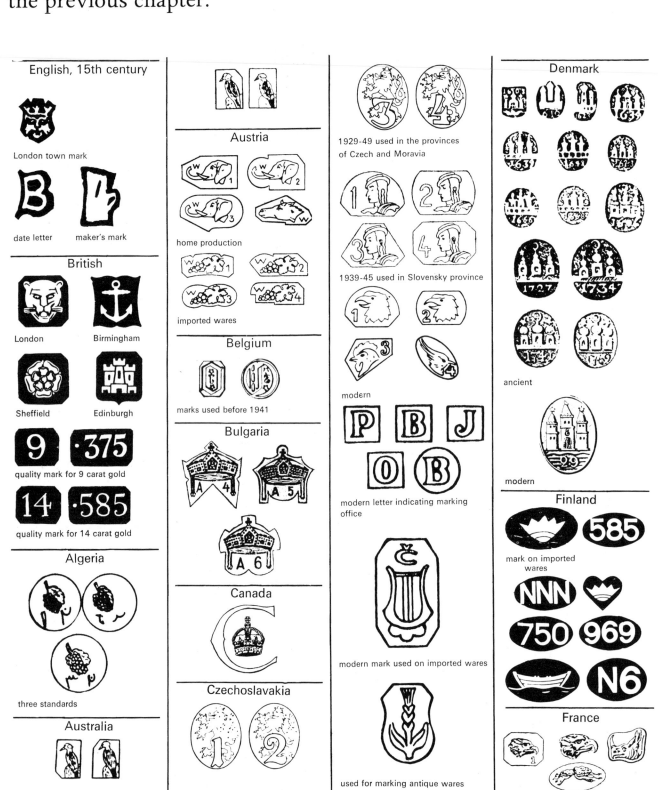

English, 15th century

London town mark

date letter   maker's mark

British

London   Birmingham

Sheffield   Edinburgh

quality mark for 9 carat gold

quality mark for 14 carat gold

Algeria

three standards

Australia

Austria

home production

imported wares

Belgium

marks used before 1941

Bulgaria

Canada

Czechoslovakia

1929-49 used in the provinces of Czech and Moravia

1939-45 used in Slovensky province

modern

modern letter indicating marking office

modern mark used on imported wares

used for marking antique wares

Denmark

ancient

modern

Finland

mark on imported wares

France

Hungary

Austro-Hungarian Empire, 1866-1937

modern

Israel

Irish

Italy

Malta

Netherlands

pre-1953, M is date letter for 1900,
V for 1905

pre-1953, small articles

pre-1953, small articles of
quality 583/1000

modern, R is date letter for 1952-3

modern marks used on imported
wares

small articles

Norway

Poland

Portugal

800

Romania

Sweden

Switzerland

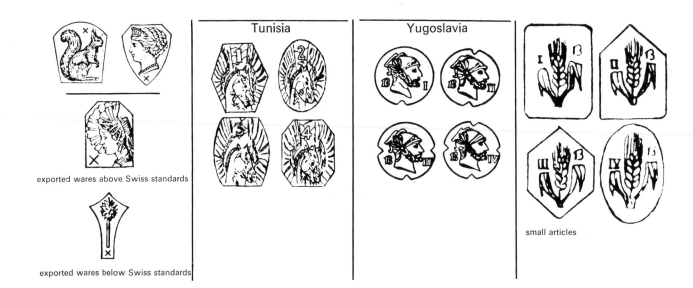

Tunisia

Yugoslavia

exported wares above Swiss standards

exported wares below Swiss standards

small articles

A 16th-century jeweller's workshop. Left: *an apprentice draws wire on a drawbench.* Centre: *the craftsmen have leather aprons to catch the gold fragments taken off by the tools.* Right: *a craftsman anneals his work in a furnace.*

Glossary

acanthus   leaf ornament derived from the capital of a Corinthian column

aigrette   a hair ornament

alloy   a metal mixed with others. Sometimes for economic reasons but more usually to obtain different working qualities or to vary the colour.

annealing   process of restoring the malleability of a metal. When metal is hammered to work it, its atomic structure is changed and it becomes hard and brittle. It is annealed by heating and quenching it. This operation calls for a critical control of temperature, otherwise the work will melt away on the hearth. The ancient smiths did this visually, and the practice of annealing in the darkest corner of the workshop is still common. In the gloom it is easier to judge the colour, and hence the temperature, of the work in the flame, and to know the right moment to remove it.

anthemion   stylised honeysuckle decoration used in the Adam period and derived from Roman murals unearthed at Herculaneum and Pompeii

assay   to try a metal, i.e. to test its purity

baluster   a form derived from the pillars of a balustrade

Baroque   rich late Renaissance decoration

basse-taille   a refinement of champlevé enamelling. A shaded effect is achieved by varying the depth of the intaglio cutting in the metal. The Royal Gold Cup of France, now in the British Museum, has basse-taille enamelling of superb quality.

bezel   a metal flange, turned over to keep a gemstone in a box setting

carat   measure of the fineness of gold. Pure gold is 24 carat; 18 carat has 18 parts in 24 of pure gold, and so on. Not to be confused with the carat-weight of gemstones, which derived from the use in early times of the seeds of the carob tree for weighing stones. Today the metric carat is equivalent to 0.2 of a gramme.

cartouche   ornamental scroll usually designed to contain a coat-of-arms or monogram

cast chasing   type of chasing done on castings to tidy them up, brighten them and give them life

casting   method of producing forms by pouring or throwing molten gold into a hollow mould. The sand caster made models in wood or clay, pressed one between two boxfuls of sand mixed with oil, removed the model and clamped the boxes together again. They now had a hollow mould. Pre-Columbian goldsmiths in South and Central America made open moulds by carving out a slab of stone.

Lost-wax casting, developed by the Egyptians, has been used intermittently by goldsmiths for 5,000 years. A wax model is placed in an open-ended can with a sprue or vent. In the past it may have been surrounded with wet clay but nowadays a substance like plaster of Paris is employed. When this has set, the can is placed in an oven. The melted wax pours out of the sprue and is 'lost'. If molten gold is forced into the mould while on a centrifuge the force drives it into the fine detail. In Britain, Michael Ayrton and John Donald, after much experiment, cast a gold honeycomb from a real one by treating the comb as a wax model.

casting on   method of attaching terminals, e.g. to torcs. Moulds are wired to the unfinished ends of the piece, or a collar mould is made by the lost-wax process and placed between a separately made terminal and the piece itself. When molten gold is poured in it forms a welding collar or a terminal.

caudle cup   a 17th-century two-handled cup made

to hold thin oatmeal gruel flavoured with wine or ale, sugar and spice

champlevé enamel one of the most effective enamel techniques. An intaglio pattern is cut in the metal with gravers and the recesses filled with enamel. Cellini advised spreading it with a small copper palette knife. The piece is then placed in an oven for the enamel to fuse, and the cycle is repeated for another coat. Finally the surface is scoured with stone or sand and polished with tripoli, a limestone powder.

chasing the first method to be evolved for decorating the surface of gold. A painting of about 1380 B.C. shows an Egyptian chaser working on a golden sphinx. The modern chaser supports his work by filling it with pitch. Then he draws out the design on the surface of the metal and delineates it with a hammer and punches, not removing metal but pushing it aside. Chasing is very slow. It takes about 300 hours to chase the feathers on a pheasant.

chinoiserie form of decoration derived from oriental art. Popular in the Charles II period and again in the mid-18th century.

cloisons receptacles for gem material or enamel, created by soldering gold strips on to a backing

cloisonné enamel earliest enamelling technique. A web of gold strips soldered to a gold plate is filled with enamel. The effect is stiffer than champlevé and has been likened to stained glass, because the intersection of the strips resembles that of the leads in a church window.

coloured golds white gold is obtained by alloying with nickel or palladium; red by increasing the copper content; blue by adding iron; purple by adding aluminium; mauve by alloying with zinc; and green by alloying with silver and cadmium.

cupellation an assaying method. The sample is wrapped in lead, placed in the hollow of a cupel, or refractory block, and put in an oven. When the lead melts it carries the base metal oxides into the porous block. The gold and any silver in it are left.

drawplate a plate with holes in it, or sometimes with diamond dies inserted. Used for reducing and shaping wire. The ancient goldsmith would first have had to hammer out ingots into thin rods (these are produced today between grooved rolls in mechanical presses). Next, the end was tapered and the rod winched back and forth through a succession of holes in the drawplate, each smaller than the one before. The wires used by the Greeks in filigree were often not much thicker than a human hair.

electro-plating process patented in 1840 by G. R. Elkington for producing simulated gold jewellery with a thin surface deposit of gold. The article to be plated acts as the cathode in an electrolytic cell filled with a solution containing gold potassium cyanide. When a current is passed through the cell, the gold atoms in the solution are attracted to the cathode and adhere to it. Early electroplating could only be applied thinly or holes would form in the deposit. New solutions and baths with controlled current density enable plate to be deposited today to virtually any thickness without flaws. Pieces have been produced in Scandinavia with so much gold on them that they could be assayed as nine carat.

electrum alloy of gold and silver. Much of the electrum used in ancient times was a natural alloy.

enamel glass powdered in a pestle and mortar, then suspended in water so that it can be painted on a gold surface. It is then fired in a furnace to re-fuse the glass. Colours are obtained by mixing in metallic oxides.

engraving engraved decoration consists of scoring lines into the surface with a sharp graver. The metal is cut away, not pushed aside as in chasing. The characteristics of engraving are a freedom of expression implicit in the rapid, firm strokes which must be made if the cutting is to be even, and the brightness on the edges of the lines (though years of use may, of course, polish this away). Engraving tends to be very good or very bad. Compare the superb engraving of the feathery heraldic crests on Caroline work with the weak drawing of the chinoiserie engraving in the same period.

faience glazed ceramic used for beads or inlays in jewellery

false filigree effects produced by casting from a filigree model, as practised by the Mixtec gold workers in pre-Columbian Mexico

filigree decorative work composed of fine wire. The Hellenistic Greeks excelled in this work. Patience and dexterity are required in the twisting and soldering of the hair-like gold wires.

finial the ornament surmounting a gold ware

flatwares plates and trays, spoons and forks, etc.

fluting semi-circular vertical channels like those in classical columns. When the makers of the Ipswich torcs drew down their rods from gold bars, an adjustable key was probably inserted into the drawing die. When the rod was winched through the die, the key scribed a flute down its length.

foil a thin leaf of metal alloy placed behind a gemstone to set it off and improve its colour. Cellini, discussing the making of foils in his *Treatise on Goldsmithing*, advises that the metal first be beaten to 'about the thickness of two knifebacks'. Then, ensuring that his hammer was smooth and burnished, he is to beat it as thin as he can, 'blanc clean and polish it' and finally burnish the surface with a graver. All this for a piece of foil that will be laid in a setting and never seen again.

gilding applying a gold surface to another substance, usually silver or copper. The earliest technique was to bond thin gold plates to the other metal by glueing or heating. When making large objects, craftsmen often did this to economise on gold. Tutankhamun's outer sarcophagus, for instance, was of wood plated with gold, and many plated silver vessels were found at Mycenae. Another early technique employed niello as the bonding agent. The curious affinity of gold for mercury led to mercurial gilding, used by Renaissance smiths to make their monumental silver wares look like gold. An amalgam of gold and mercury was painted on the vessel, which was then heated until the mercury evaporated, leaving a film of gold. Gilt bronze work was produced at many periods in Europe. Nowadays gilding is carried out by electro-plating (see above).

gimmel ring ring formed by two hoops slotted together. The loops were sometimes worn separately as betrothal rings.

granulation small spheres of gold applied to a gold surface as decoration, generally in rows, pyramids or clusters. The Etruscans used spheres 1/1000th of an inch in diameter, formed either by heating pieces of gold between layers of powdered charcoal in a crucible or by dropping molten gold on a marble slab. The bond used by these masters of granulation to hold the spheres in place has not been identified. It may have contained copper salts to produce the final bond by colloid hard soldering.

hallmarks marks struck on precious metals to show that they have been assayed and are up to standard.

holloware a metal ware of hollow form, such as a cup or a bowl. The Sumerian smiths were as adept at making gold vessels as anyone working today. They would have scribed a circle on gold sheet cutting out the disc with a hammer and bronze chisel. The disc was laid on a section of tree trunk with a recess in it. Hammering from the perimeter inward, the smith produced a gold saucer shape.

Placing this on a raising-stake, he hammered it again until he had a cup, jug or beaker shape. The raising of the body of a vessel from a disc takes a craftsman a whole working day, and he will spend another going over the surface with a small planishing hammer which evens out the raising marks and imparts a subtle patina. Feet, handles and spout are soldered on afterwards. Other vessel-making techniques are 'folding' – bending sheet into a tube form and soldering along the seam, as in Queen Anne coffee pots – and soldering separately hammered halves together, as in early boat-shaped dishes.

intaglio pattern cut into gold with a graver

knop boss on stem of a cup, chalice, candlestick

lunulae sickle-shaped pendants produced by ancient British smiths

matting textured chased decoration produced with a special matting punch

mount gold or silver decoration affixed to another object, often a casting

niello diminutive of *niger*. Black decoration on gold, popular in Roman times. First a black compound was mixed, often of silver, copper, lead and sulphur. It was hammered out, powdered and then painted into intaglio-cut patterns in the surface. Finally it was fused in an oven.

opus interrasile Roman and Byzantine pierced decoration done with hammer and punches.

parure matching suite of jewellery

pectoral a jewel or gold plate worn on the breast

piercing decoration produced by cutting through the metal with hammer and chisel, a fret-saw or press tools. Modern manufacturing silversmiths and goldsmiths place punches in a power press and achieve in seconds what it would have taken a craftsman with a hammer hours to accomplish.

pinchbeck substitute for gold invented by Christopher Pinchbeck, a London watchmaker, in 1732. It consisted of 83 parts copper and 17 zinc. Workshops in London and Birmingham turned out a variety of wares in this cheap metal.

plique-à-jour variation on cloisonné enamel. The cloisons have no backs, and the enamel is built up in relief above the walls of the open frames. As the absence of backing allows more light to pass through the enamel, this work is even more like stained-glass windows than conventional cloisonné. Cellini's method when working in plique-à-jour was to lay out his gold strip on a bed of clay with an iron plate underneath. After the cloisons had been filled with enamel and fired to fuse it, he broke away the clay backing

pressing similar to stamping (see below) except that an hydraulic or power press is used

raising creating a hollow form in metal by hammering it up from flat sheet. See *holloware*.

refining purifying a precious metal by removing alien metals. In gold, the main ones are silver and copper.

repoussé relief decoration, produced by hammering. If it is done from the back of the surface, the design is brought up. If it is done from the front, the background is pushed down around the pattern. On enclosed forms like teapots, where there is a difficulty in direct hammering, a tool called the snarling iron is used. It is an elongated steel Z, on one end of which a small dome is formed. This end is placed inside the vessel and the other end is clamped in a vice. When the straight arm of the tool is hit with a hammer, the resulting vibration beats out the relief. This remote control hammering is believed to have been used in Peru as early as A.D. 100 to produce cups in the form of human heads.

The term repoussé chasing, often met with in books and sale-room catalogues, describes repoussé work which has been chased with punches after the basic pattern has been hammered up.

Rococo derived from *rocaille,* meaning rock-like. This style was evolved in France. Its characteristics are asymmetry and riotous decorative detail.

rolled gold simulated gold sheet, wire and tube, consisting of base metal with a gold surface. In the 18th century Thomas Bolsover fused silver and copper, whose melting point is lower when they are in conjunction than when either metal is pure. He rolled the resulting bimetallic block into sheet with a silver surface, now known as Old Sheffield Plate. The technique was applied to gold in 1817.

setting the claws, or box, by which a gem is secured to a piece of jewellery. Ancient Egyptian jewellers used cloison settings. They soldered lengths of gold strip to the backing plate to form a web of channels. Lapis lazuli, turquoises and cornelians were cut to fit the design, placed in the spaces and held in position by 'rubbing' the top edge of the gold strip over the sides of the stones with a graver. Later, when diamonds, emeralds, rubies and sapphires were used, the jewellers gave them greater prominence by soldering on individual little box settings for them. They were still held in by the rub-over method, which was used until the 18th century. Sometimes the turned-over edge was tooled with fine patterns, and these variations are known as millegraine or thread settings.

The 10th-century monk-goldsmith who made the Holy Roman emperor's crown was far ahead of his time in setting innovations. He used boxes of filigree and held in the stones with little bird's-foot claws. This method let much more light into the stones than the enclosed box settings and anticipated the modern collette setting, which looks like a little openwork crown.

The stones on Princess Blanche's beautiful wedding crown, made about 1400, were brought forward from the uprights on long settings that made the whole piece resemble a wreath of flowers. See also *foil*.

shank the hoop of a ring

smallworker a maker of vertu, such as small boxes

smelting melting gold and passing a current of oxygen over it. This induces the base metal impurities to form oxides which float on the gold as scum that can be ladled off.

spinning creating a hollow form from metal sheet by turning on a lathe

stamping creating a metal ware by pressing it between a male and female die in a stamping press or fly-press

troy weight a troy pound is made up of 12 ounces, each of 20 pennyweights. The troy pound is equivalent to 13.164 ounces avoirdupois.

twentieth-century techniques the ancient goldsmiths had to fabricate their own sheet, wire and tube from the gold ingots they obtained from the royal treasuries. Nowadays refiners supply them with these materials, made to precise tolerances and mirror-finished by polished rolls and hardened steel dies.

As for decoration, mechanised engraving is now done by engine-turning machines which break up the surface of the gold with a wide variety of straight-line and wavy patterns. Diamond milling consists of milling the surface with a diamond instead of a steel graver to produce a series of very bright facets. Diamond milled designs tend to be rather monotonous.

Textured gold is replacing the vogue for brightness. Jewellers and goldsmiths now use a flexible drill and the same tools as dentists to produce textured effects. A technique developed by Fabergé, which has become popular again, is to heat a completed piece in a flame so that the gold runs on the surface. The result is a finish that looks like the substance in which gold originated – molten lava.

Bibliography

ASCAIN, A., and ARNAUD, J. M., *Histoire de la Monnaie et de la Finance*, Edito-Service, Geneva, 1965.
BARSALI, Isa Belli, *Medieval Goldsmiths' Work*, Paul Hamlyn, London, 1969.
BARSALI, Isa Belli, *European Enamels*, Paul Hamlyn, London, 1969.
BECKER, Thomas W., *The Coin Makers*, The Oak Tree Press, London, 1969, Doubleday, New York, 1969.
BERTON, Pierre, *The Golden Trail*, Macmillan, Toronto, 1954.
BRADFORD, E., *Victorian Jewellery*, Country Life, London, 1953.
BRADFORD, E., *Four Centuries of European Jewellery*, Heywood, London, 1950, Philosophical Library, New York, 1953.
BROOKE, G. C., *English Coins*, Methuen, London, 1950.
CUSS, T. P. Camerer, *The Country Life Book of Watches*, Country Life, London, 1967.
CARTWRIGHT, A. P., *The Gold Miners*, Purnell, Capetown, 1962.
CARTWRIGHT, A. P., *Gold Paved the Way*, Macmillan, London, 1967.
CARTWRIGHT, A. P., *The Golden Age*, Purnell, Capetown, 1968.
CELLINI, *The Life of Benvenuto Cellini*, Phaidon Press, London, 1949, Fine Edition Press, Cleveland, USA, 1952.
CLUTTON, Cecil, and DANIELS, George, *Watches*, Batsford, London, 1965.
COTTRELL, Leonard, *The Anvil of Civilisation*, Faber & Faber, London, 1958, New American Library, New York, 1959.
COTTRELL, Leonard, *The Penguin Book of Lost Worlds*, Penguin Books, London, 1966.
COTTRELL, Leonard, *The Lion Gate*, Pan Books, London, 1967.
COTTRELL, Leonard, *The Land of Shinar*, Pan Books, London, 1968.
COTTRELL, Leonard, *The Bull of Minos*, Pan Books, London, 1969.
COTTRELL, Leonard, *The Lost Pharaohs*, Pan Books, London, 1969.
CULICAN, William, *The Medes and Persians*, Thames & Hudson, London, 1965.
EMMERICH, André, *Sweat of the Sun and Tears of the Moon*, University of Washington Press, Seattle, 1965.
EVANS, Joan, *A History of Jewellery*, Faber & Faber, London, 1953.
FALKINER, Richard, *Investing in Antique Jewellery*, Barrie and Rockliff, the Cresset Press, London, 1968, Clarkson N. Potter, New York, 1968.
GREEN, Timothy, *The World of Gold*, Michael Joseph, London, 1968, Walker, New York, 1968.
GREGORIETTI, Guido, *Jewellery Through the Ages*, Paul Hamlyn, London, 1969.
HENRY, Françoise, *Irish Art in the Early Christian Period (To A.D. 800)*, Methuen, London, 1940 (2nd Edition, 1947).
HERODOTUS, *The Histories*, Penguin Books, London, 1941.
HIGGINS, R. A., *Greek and Roman Jewellery*, Methuen, London, 1961.
INNES, Hammond, *The Conquistadores*, Collins, London, 1969, Knopf, New York, 1969.
JACKSON, C. J., *English Goldsmiths and Their Marks*, Dover, London, 1965.
JAQUET, Eugene, and CHAPUIS, Alfred, *Technique and History of the Swiss Watch*, Spring Books, London, 1970.
LAVENDER, David, *The American West*, Penguin Books and American Heritage Publishing Co, London and New York, 1969.
LISTER, Raymond, *The Craftsman in Metal*, G. Bell & Sons, London, 1966, A. S. Barnes, New Jersey, USA, 1968.
LLOYD, Seton, *Early Highland People of Anatolia*, Thames & Hudson, London, 1967, McGraw-Hill, New York, 1967.
DESROCHES NOBLECOURT, Christiane, *Tutankhamen*, The Connoisseur and Michael Joseph, London, 1963.
PHILLIPS, E. D., *The Royal Hordes*, Thames & Hudson, London, 1965.
PORTEOUS, John, *Coins*, Weidenfeld & Nicholson, London, 1964.
PRESCOTT, William H., *The Conquest of Mexico*, Everyman, London and New York, 1957.
PRESCOTT, William H., *The Conquest of Peru*, Everyman, London and New York, 1963.
ROSS, Anne, *Everyday Life of the Pagan Celts*, Batsford, London, 1970, Putnam, New York, 1970.
SCHOLZ, Renate, *Jagdlicher Schmuck*, Paul Parey, Berlin, 1970.
SMITH, William Stevenson, *The Art and Architecture of Ancient Egypt*, Penguin Books, London, 1950.
SNOWMAN, Abraham Kenneth, *The Art of Carl Fabergé*, Faber & Faber, London, 1962, Boston Book and Art Shop, Boston, 1953.
SNOWMAN, Abraham Kenneth, *Eighteenth-Century Gold Boxes of Europe*, Faber & Faber, London, 1966, Boston Book and Art Shop, Boston, 1966.
SOUSTELLE, Jacques, *The Daily Life of the Aztecs*, Weidenfeld & Nicholson, London, 1961.
STRONG, D. E., *Greek and Roman Gold and Silver Plate*, Methuen, London, 1966.
SUTHERLAND, C. H. V., *Gold*, Thames & Hudson, London, 1959, McGraw-Hill, New York, 1959.
TWINING, Lord, *The History of the Crown Jewels of Europe*, Batsford, London, 1960.
UNTRACHT, Oppi, *Metal Techniques for Craftsmen*, Robert Hale, London, 1969.
VILMOKOVA, Milada, and DARBOIS, Dominique, *Egyptian Jewellery*, Paul Hamlyn, London, 1969.
WOOLLEY, Sir Leonard, *Ur Excavations*, Oxford University Press, Oxford, 1927.
WOOLLEY, Sir Leonard, *The Development of Sumerian Art*, Faber & Faber, London, 1935.
ZARATE, Augustin de, *The Discovery and Conquest of Peru*, Penguin Books, London, 1968.

*Holbein's design for a cup presented to Jane Seymour by Henry VIII. Ashmolean
Museum, Oxford.*

Index

Numbers in *italic* refer to the captions.

Abydos 50
Achaemenid bowls 80
Achelous 73
Adelaide of England 186
Adrian I, Pope 99
Aegina Treasure 67, *68*
Agamemnon 64, 73
Agilulf, Cross of 93
Agincourt, Battle of 179
Agricola 21, *22*
Alaca Huyuk 64
Alaska 42
Albert, Gilbert *165*, 170
Alexander the Great 11, 30, 79, 84, 200
Alexandra of Russia *169*, 169
Alexis Michael of Russia 194
Alfred Jewel *109*
Algeria 207
Alisida Treasure 69
Alps 30, 32
Amenemhet 55
Amenhotep III of Egypt 57
Amenophis III of Egypt 26
Amenpnufer 26–7
America 203
American River 37, 39
Amiens cathedral 188
Amon-Re 69
Ampelta, vase of 58
Anatolia 47, 64, 67
Anderson, Charlie 45
Andes 34
Andrieu *180*
Anglo-Saxons 201
Ann of Cleves 122
Anne of England 179
   style of *138*, 157, 217
Appalachian Indians *23*, 24
Appleby, Malcolm *173*
Apollo 200
   shrine of *28*
Aquinas, St Thomas 46
Arabs 31, 32, 68
Ardagh Chalice *104*, 105
Ardys of Lydia 28, 199
Argentina 207
Argonauts 21
Aristotle 46, 69, 115
Armada 36
   Jewel, the *150*
Arno 69
Arsinoe I of Egypt *180*
Arsinoe II of Egypt *180*, 200
Art Nouveau 159ff, *160*, *167*
Ashanti *131*, 131–2, 133
Ashcroft Trail 45
Asia 21
Asprey 168

Assyria 26, 62, 69, 75
Atahualpa 33, 34, 127
Athelney *109*
Athena, statue of 80
Athens 28, 199
   National Museum at 64
Aucoc, Louis 160
Aumale, Duke of 110
Australia 12, 14, 36, 39, 207
Austria 207
Avars 31
Axholme, Lincolnshire 102
Ayrton, Michael 215
Aztecs 32, 33, 125, *126*, 127
Babylon 9, 26, 27, 62, 79
Baghdad 31
Bamberg 192
Bank of England 37
   of France 37
Barbarians 93, 95, 200
Barfield, Sue *173*
Barnato Brothers 41
Baroque 157, 158, 215
Barrière 188
Batavia *158*
Bathurst 39
Bavaria, Empress of 192
Beatty, Sir Chester *144*
Beit, Alfred 40
Belgium 167, 207
Belshazzar 27, 63
Bennett, Lake 45
Benney, Gerald *149*, *170*
Berenice 8, 25
Berker, Friedrich 170
Berne 211
Bernhardt, Sarah 166
Berps 212
Berri, Duc de 113
Bexley hoard 102
Big Bonanza mine 39
Birmingham 154, 206, 207, 217
Black Prince's ruby 179
Black Sea 21
Blanche, Princess, crown of 110, *111*, 192
Blerzy, Joseph Etienne *121*
Blood, Colonel 179
Boccacio 116
Bohemia 32, 189, 208
Bolivia 205
Bologna 203
Bolsover, Thomas 218
Bonanza Creek *43*
Borgias 122
Botticelli 116
Boucher 147
Boulton, Matthew 154
Bourget, Jean 149
Boyne, River 105
Bradbury, Frederick 206
Bramante, Donato 202

Bratislava 208
Brazil 36, 135, *180*, 204
Brembarti, Isotta 123
Brindisi, Augustale 201
Britain 12, 50, 92, 102, 154, 170, 206
Brno 208
Buddhist reliquary 133
Bulgaria 80, 83, 207
Burma *134*, 134
Burton, Capt. F. C. 78
Bucharest 93
Byzantium 8, 31, 63, 87, 93, 97, 177, 200, 204, 217
   coins of *98*
   style of 99, 101, 133, 186, 188, 192, 195, 196, 207
Caceres 69
Cadiz 30, 69
Cairo Museum 51
Cajamarca, battle of 33, 34
Calais Noble, the *180*
California 10, 12, *24*, 36–40, 63
Canaanites 62, 68
Canada 42, 207
Canning Jewel *123*, 124
Carlisle 92
Carnarvon, Lord 55
Carter, Howard 55–7, 59
Carthage 10, 30, 69, 75, 84, *180*
Cartier 168
Catherine I of Russia 192
Cellini, B. 124, 203, 216, 218
Celtic 48, 76, 93, 102, *104*, 104
Cézanne, Paul 159
Charlemagne 31, 186
Charles I of England 13, 155, *180*, 209, 216
Charles II of England 155, 179, 186, 200, 203
Charles IV of Bohemia 189
Charles V of France 178
Charles VIII of Sweden 197
Charles IX of Sweden 198
Charles the Bold 177
Chartres cathedral 110
Chavin Indians 50, 127
Cheops of Egypt 51
Chester 206
Chilkoot Pass 45
Chimu 128
China 135–6, *136*, 147
Chirico, Giorgio di 170
Circle City 42
Classical 144
Classical revival 157
Columbia 9
Columbus, Christopher 32
Commonwealth 155, 156, 178
Comstock, Harry 39
Comstock's Lode 39
Cong, Cross of 105–6, *106*
Conquistadores 9
Conrad II, Holy Roman Emperor 186
Constance of Aragon 195